ONE HEART
AT A TIME

Delilah

Paperback edition published 2020 by RosettaBooks

ISBN-13 (paperback): 978-1-9481-2256-6
ISBN-13 (hardcover): 978-1-9481-2216-0
ISBN-13 (ebook): 978-1-9481-2215-3

Cover design by Mumtaz Mustafa
Cover photo by Brandon Hill
Interior design by Alexia Garaventa

Library of Congress Cataloging-in-Publication Data

Names: Delilah, 1960- author.
Title: One heart at a time / Delilah.
Description: Trade paperback edition. | New York : RosettaBooks, 2020. |
Identifiers: LCCN 2019046935 | ISBN 9781948122566 (trade paperback)
Subjects: LCSH: Delilah, 1960- | Radio broadcasters--
United States--Biography.
Classification: LCC PN1991.4.D455 A3 2020 | DDC 791.4402/8092 [B]--dc23
LC record available at https://lccn.loc.gov/2019046935

www.RosettaBooks.com
Printed in Canada

RosettaBooks®

CONTENTS

FOREWORD

When I was approached by the owners of our hometown AM radio station back in 1974, and asked if I'd like to do on-air school reports once a week, I had no idea that moment would lead to the only career I've ever had. Over forty-five years later, countless radio stations, and thirty-six years of hosting my own radio program, playing your song requests, and dispensing homegrown snippets of advice to listeners, I still feel the same thrill that fourteen-year-old girl felt the first time the ON AIR light went on, and her voice went out over the airwaves. I love what I do.

My parents named me Delilah. It was a somewhat exotic moniker to place on a child of the '60s and I've always felt a little bit different than the crowd because of it. Perhaps that's part of the reason I'm an attention seeker—something those radio station owners knew, and because they were good men who cared about others and their community, they thought to channel my youthful energies into a more healthful and productive activity than other things I could have gotten up to. How grateful I am for that! Gratitude is the overarching theme of my program, and hopefully the big takeaway of my listening audience.

When I travel to Ghana, West Africa, to work with Point Hope, an organization I founded in 2004 helping refugees, the elderly, disabled, and vulnerable local populations gain access to things we take for granted, like food, clean water, and health care, I am brought to my knees by the circumstances in which the people of that nation live, and I am so very grateful for my life!

I have a crazy love for children and don't think I'll ever have an empty nest. I welcomed my fourteenth child in 2019, a teenage girl from the US foster system, and two new grandchildren joined our ever-growing family. Finding matching Christmas pajamas is getting more difficult! My family flowchart doesn't follow any of the standards folks are used to; my three-year-old son is an uncle to my seventeen-year-old granddaughter! Whenever I encounter a child who needs a family, they'll likely find one with me.

With my radio show, my podcast series, *LOVE SOMEONE with Delilah*, speaking engagements, kids and grandkids to love on, farm animals to care for, and acres of gardens to tend to… I'll admit, sometimes I grapple with my own on-air advice to "slow down and love someone." Yet, I remind myself that everything I do is a choice and I am so very grateful that I have the options and the choices and the life that I lead.

I strive to be a voice of light in the darkness. We need to focus on all the light, love, and compassion in our world, lest the dark and divisiveness (the images our mainstream media makes big money on convincing us is the only news out there) take root in our soul. "A house divided will not long stand." Why are we fighting against our brothers and sisters, instead of building bridges of understanding? I'm all about connection, and hope to help others see the many things we have in common and can celebrate in one another. This is more important than ever right now!

The growth of the overall disconnectedness and abject loneliness of people during the last two decades lies heavy on my heart. I hear it from callers all the time and almost every person I've talked to who has ever attempted suicide says the same thing: they felt utterly and completely alone, unable to bear the weight of the sadness from their depression and isolation. I'm not a stranger to grief and sorrow myself, and I can often hear my own worries reflected in the voices of my callers. I don't always know what to say, but I think I know what to do. It's simple, we need to change the world. We need to flip the switch, shift our focus, and zero in on what's important. People and hearts and compassion. Gratitude.

So how do we change the world? One Heart at a Time.

I'll start by sharing my personal stories and what I've learned in my experiences, the positive and the negative, my hope is you'll start to see the miracles in your own life, recognize divine promptings, consider your purpose, follow with prayerful obedience, open yourself to serve others, and let go of things that burden you—all so you may find peace in this sometimes harsh existence.

When your life comes into harmony with the Lord's plan for you, and people around you start to notice the change, guess what? They'll want to know what you know. So you'll share your stories too, soften hearts, open eyes, and change the world with me, One Heart at a Time.

Delilah
January, 2020

CHAPTER I:
A HEART RESTORED

I believe in miracles. The everyday natural wonders of creation that go unnoticed more often than not. Miracles like a fat, grubby caterpillar climbing a slender branch, decimating the existing vegetation, wrapping itself in layers of thread it creates from its little body, sleeping for a few weeks, and after chewing its way out of the bed sack, emerging a breathtaking winged thing. As a butterfly, it then takes flight and travels for thousands of miles to a destination it has never seen. How the heck do they know to fly thousands of miles to Mexico?

I also believe in big miracles. Moses parting the Red Sea, the blind seeing again, and even breath coming back into a lifeless body—the type of miracles you mostly only hear or read about. I wasn't raised or taught to believe in them, per se. My mom sent us to Bible camp just to get us out of the house in the long summer months, not because she or Dad believed in what we were being taught (while we made decoupage plaques of a blond-haired, blue-eyed Jesus from playing cards). I believe in big miracles because I witnessed one when I was a child, and it is burned in my mind forever.

My home state is known for its long rainy season. Inland Oregon is a dry desert environment, but the coastal region is a big, green sponge that never really dries out. Out of this sponge grow some of the tallest trees in the world, the Douglas firs and the great sequoias, the famous redwoods that ten men holding hands could not encompass. When I was a toddler, we lived on a farm surrounded by fields that walked right up to the edge of the great forests, but did not step a foot in. The forests met the fields where there was a stream connecting the two, inhabited by frogs, salamanders, tadpoles, and crawdads that I caught on every occasion.

Before catch and release became a popular style of fishing, my brother Matt and I did that nearly every day with the creatures we caught. The stream was home to a breed of salamander known as water doggies, or Oregon rough-skinned newts, their official name. They look like tiny brown lab puppies, with long tails. Adorably cute, their big eyes would stare back at me just like a dog's, and their skin is both soft and rough at the same time. They were fun to catch and handle and watch as they curled up in the palm of my chubby hand. Their undersides are orange, and it's this bright underside that makes them famous. Their skin contains a poison called tetrodotoxin, or TTX, that, if consumed, will kill you. It is ten thousand times more toxic than a shot of cyanide. I don't remember worrying about this fact as a kid, but I suppose it's one of the reasons Mom made us wash our hands before dinner.

Spring had morphed into a sweet, mild summer and my parents were cleaning out the basement of our rental house. My job, at five years old, was to sweep the cement floor and carry the rubbish to the top of the basement stairs and dump it in the burning barrel. As I reached my chubby hands into the mesh drain guard in the cement floor, I found a dead water doggie. I pulled it out and held its cute face close to my own. Its eyes were closed, its body shriveled to about a third of its normal size. It was as hard as a rock and curled in the shape of a C. It had crawled into the drain, gotten stuck in the mesh grate, and dried out when the winter rains stopped. I showed it to Mom, who told me to throw it away and wash my hands. Dad didn't even look up from his project but echoed the same instructions.

I remember praying—I have no idea where I learned to pray, but I did—then I set the dehydrated water doggie on the ledge of cement at the top of the stairs. I simply asked God to make it live again. I was so sad that it had shriveled up, and I was determined to put it back in the creek next to the house. I went and got a pail, put a couple inches of water in the bottom, carried it back to the cement, and dropped the water doggie in. The memory of what happened in the next ten minutes is burned in my mind forever, as I watched the hardened creature begin to relax out of its curved shape and start to move. I screamed and jumped and screamed some more. My parents thought I had gotten hurt, I was making so much noise, and both came bounding up the cement stairs to see why I was so loud. There in the bottom of the bucket was a wiggling, moving, eyes-opened water doggie…

Okay, maybe not as impressive as a stone being rolled away from a tomb, but to me it was proof positive that A) God listened to my prayers and B) He could bring things back to life.

I put the salamander back in the creek, and then I started to pray for animals constantly. Living on a farm gave me ample opportunity to do so. I prayed when Mom took the hatchet to the chicken coop that we wouldn't have fried chicken and gravy for dinner. I prayed when a calf was born too early that it would survive. When my dog Dusty got hit by a motorcycle, I prayed that she would live despite her broken back. Sadly, we had chicken and gravy at least once a week, and I missed a week of school from crying too much when Dusty died.

But on one other occasion, my prayers were answered. A small barn owl had crashed into my grandma's front window and was lying on the ground. I prayed it was just stunned, knocked out from the impact, but after an hour or more of my praying and coaxing, the bird was still lifeless and had turned cold in my hands. Grandma and I thought it was so beautiful, she decided to give it to our neighbor who was a taxidermist. We put it in a coffee can and stuck it in the pantry freezer. Later, needing room for some baked goods, she took the owl in the coffee can out and set it on top of the chest freezer. About an hour later, I heard a noise in the pantry and went to see what it was. The coffee can had fallen off the freezer and was moving on the floor. When I picked it up, I heard a noise inside and was so startled I dropped it again. Then I grabbed the can and ran to Grandma, who peeked inside to find the owl quite alive. We released it back in the barn, and after about half an hour of stumbling, falling, and getting back up, the owl spread its wings and flew.

⌒〜〇

My world shattered a year ago on October 2, 2017. That night, my beautiful son, Zachariah Miguel Rene-Ortega, the last child I carried in my womb and gave birth to, chose to leave us. He was just eighteen years old. These have been the hardest months of my life, and that of my family. I miss him every minute and hour of every day. Despite the heartache and grief, I praise God for the life I live. I know that God is looking after us, and that, along with the love and understanding of family, friends, and so many others has kept me going.

Right now, our hearts are big and raw and sore from the absence of him, and my memories block out the reality of most days bringing choking sobs every night. It is breath by breath, step by step, that I move through the days without my Zack Attack. We speak openly of Zack, of missing him like we do, and how his heart impacted all of our lives. He, like his brother Sammy, are in the arms of our Savior—of that I am sure. But I cannot help but want them here, in my arms. These arms that ache to hold them, to stroke their hair, to make their favorite foods.

Both knew and loved their Father, and He knew their hearts. For whatever childhood struggles and teen angst they experienced, theirs were hearts that made a difference in this world even in the all too short time they were with us.

One of my most endearing memories of my Zacky that illustrates what his one heart was truly like and truly capable of starts off in a mountain cabin surrounded by snow...

I stretched out on the dull, orange shag carpet, imagining what it looked like thirty years earlier when it was new. My back was up against a worn couch, not as worn as the carpet but it had clearly seen better days. My daughters, Lonika, Shaylah, Angel, and Kristi along with our nanny, Malory, were in the kitchen, sitting around the stained wood table playing games and laughing.

We were all sore from the day of skiing and snowboarding, and had just eaten a hearty meal of roast beef, potatoes, carrots, and onions that I put in the crock pot before heading for a day on the slopes.

My ten-year-old son Zack was snuggled up next to me, insistent that we watch the movie *Stardust*, but nodding off in the first few minutes. Zack lives for our annual trip to the snow; being in the mountains and speeding down the slopes at full speed on his board was his favorite place to be. He was the first one awake in the morning, snow gear on, one of his many green beanies atop his tousled hair, board in his gloved hands.

In all we brought seventeen of our family members and friends up to Crystal Mountain, two hours south of Seattle. I had discovered this treasure trove of a funky cabin many seasons before, and we were lucky to get it for the Christmas break and New Year's Eve week the winter of 2009. The cabin was literally built around a massive Douglas Fir tree. The trunk of the tree was at least five feet across, and the entire cabin, all four floors, was built around its massive circumference with circular stairs wound around the pitch-encrusted bark. The first floor— usually unseen in the winter as it was buried beneath many feet of snow—is where the owners kept a separate apartment for themselves. The second story held a sauna, game room with a pool table, dart board, exercise equipment, hot tub (long defunct), and cupboards crammed with every game from chess to Yahtzee. Antique skis decorated the walls along with group photos of Olympic ski teams from decades past. The owners of the cabin were three generations of skiers.

The third floor was where we spent all our time—a big kitchen, sunken living room, two bedrooms, and the tv room where we all piled in. Outside was a wide snow-covered deck where mountain birds, especially the friendly gray jays, would eat the leftovers we put on the railing. The owners told us to hold out seeds and stand very still. Within ten minutes they would be eating from the palms of my kids' small hands.

To say the cabin was antiquated, even outdated, would have been an understatement! The kitchen appliances were the same harvest gold that had been in my folks' house, built in the 60s. The matted down shag carpeting was bright orange and the linoleum in the kitchen was a pattern I knew from my grandparents' house. Most of the other cabins from this era that had for decades sat on the side of Crystal Mountain, known as the Gold Chair area, had been torn down. New, modern multimillion-dollar winter homes with expensive snowmobiles parked in the drifts outside now stood where shabby cabins had nestled for decades. And today, nine years later, the cabin built around the tree is long gone, only our memories remain.

Zack drifted off to sleep, his red wind-burned face in my lap, before the flying ships appeared—their flamboyant captain played by Robert De Niro. He was sound asleep when the three witch sisters turned old and ugly. His favorite scene in *Stardust* is where Michele Pfeiffer, playing Lamia, casts a spell to make her sagging jowls smooth out only to have her perky breasts fall.

Our family and friends spent the night celebrating New Year's Eve with non-alcoholic champagne, board games, and lots of laughter. We spent the next day on the slopes and on January 2, a Friday, we packed up the family van and the Escalade, along with my friend Sara's car—her battery dead from several days of freezing temperatures—and we headed home, winding down the snowy mountainside. I'd taped my shows for the whole week so I didn't have to worry about getting into the studio. I anticipated a relaxing weekend to unpack and rest before the kids went back to school the following Monday.

On Saturday the phone rang and it was a girlfriend from church, letting me know that the African Children's choir was going to perform at our church on Sunday and I should make sure to bring the kids and come. I had been working in Ghana, West Africa, for five years and had adopted two beautiful young girls from Buduburam, a refugee camp. My girlfriend knew I'd love the music and even though the choir children were from a different country, my adopted girls might like seeing other children near their age from West Africa.

I spent Saturday unpacking the vehicles and trying to dry out ski bibs, jackets, gloves, boots, and pants. We lugged in the plastic totes we had filled with food and the coolers that had been packed with meats, eggs, milk, and cheese. The totes and coolers were pretty much empty and needed to be scrubbed and put away. You have no idea how insane it is to pack and unpack from a week's vacation with a family the size of ours! Each child had at least two pairs of ski gloves and two or three pair of wool socks. I spent hours trying to find the matches to about thirty-six different gloves and forty or fifty different socks! Exhausted, I tumbled into bed around midnight.

The next morning, we decided to go to the 10:30 a.m. late services. The sink was full of breakfast dishes, the living room was a makeshift laundry center for ski gear that was drying, and a week's worth of laundered towels piled on the couch. Snowboards and sleds leaned against the side of the porch.

Delilah

We made our way down near the front of the sanctuary so we could see and hear the kids perform. Their
director gave a brief message and then the music began.
Instantly I was transported ten thousand miles away to
the village I worked in. The costumes and the music lifted
me out of the church and suddenly I felt like I was back
in Ghana, caring for sick children and trying to educate
young mothers. My two daughters, Angel and Blessing,
who had been home in the US for only two years, were so
excited they could not sit still. Blessing was up and dancing in the aisle, it was all I could do to keep her from
running up on the stage to join them! Shaylah, Zack, and
Thomas were watching and swaying to the drums, clap-
ping after each song and encouraging Blessing and Angel
to dance their hearts out. The service was far too short
in our opinion, we could have listened for hours to the
rhythmic beats and chanted choruses.

After the service ended I took Angel and Blessing
to meet some of the young performers and talked with
my friend who'd called to tell me about the performance.
Paul left before me and took some of the kids back to the
farm. The director of the choir, a middle-aged man from
somewhere in the Midwest approached me with a broad
grin, grabbed my hand and started to thank me. At first I
assumed he was a listener who found out I was the woman
on the radio, and I smiled uncomfortably. But he wasn't a
listener, he was an enthusiastic choir director who pumped
my arm as he exclaimed: "Thank you! Thank you! We will
be happy to come to the farm for lunch." I tilted my head
to one side and said, "Excuse me?"

"Your son, the little boy in the green shirt just told me you have a huge farm with lots of goats and cows and then he invited me to bring the choir to lunch. Normally the church sponsors a lunch for us at the cafeteria or a local restaurant, but your pastor is not here today. I guess no one thought about how we would feed the children."

His enthusiastic smile was met with my bewildered expression, and just as I was about to explain that my house was filled with ski gear and my fridge was all but empty, Zack appeared by my side. He put his arms around me and said "Mom, I told him what a good cook you are and how you feed all the orphans in Africa, can they come home and have lunch with us?" His impish face was absolutely adorable, and his smile did to me what it always did to me, made me absolutely incapable of saying anything but "yes…"

Thirty children, eight adult chaperones, plus the director and his wife. Forty guests along with my own household of ten. My mind raced into action. I hurriedly called my then fiancé, Paul, and asked him for help. He had dropped our teenage girls off at the farm and gone to his apartment. He agreed to rush back to the farm and start picking up skis and snowboards. I called two of my adult children, Tangi and her brother Trey Jerome, who lived in the area and asked them to meet me at the church. I gave them cash and dispatched them to Walmart to buy paper plates, cups, and plastic silverware, along with rice, beans, milk, juice, spaghetti, hot dogs, and buns. Many, many hot dogs! I ordered a dozen pizzas, grabbed my youngest kids, gave the director the farm address and directions and flew out the door!

When I got home, the skis, snowboards, and damp gloves had all been snatched up and tossed in bins, the dirty dishes in the sink were shoved in the dishwasher, and a huge pot of water was already on the stove and beginning to boil. Paul started frying up sausage and hamburger for spaghetti sauce, I rinsed an entire large bag of rice (assuming the kids would enjoy it as much as my African daughters did), and tried to straighten up the bathrooms and the dining room. Within half an hour the bus arrived, and thirty children between the ages of five and eighteen started spilling out. It was freezing outside and I knew their bodies had not had time to acclimate to the cold, so they were not the least bit interested in staying outside to look at my goats, horses, or even the zebra. They all ran into the house trying to get warm, and although my house is a good size, they filled up every room.

The food was ready soon and we let the guests serve themselves. The adults went first, followed by the oldest children helping the youngest. Ten packages of Hebrew National hot dogs, ten one-pound boxes of spaghetti noodles, at least a gallon of marinara sauce, a dozen large pizzas, two huge pots of white rice, two gallons of vanilla ice cream, and two gallons of chocolate.

When everyone had eaten their fill, the kids began to perform. Even more beautiful than the songs they sang at church. Music that seemed to come from their toes and bubbled up out of their hearts filled the farm house until it seemed to sway and pulse with their unified heartbeats. Even Zack, who preferred rock and roll to soul music, tried to keep up with their dancing and singing.

After two hours of breaking bread and sharing stories and songs, the director said they had to hit the road as they had a four-hour road trip ahead. The kids gave us hugs and prayed for us, then filed out to the bus. As they rumbled up the long drive, light snow began to fall. I was ready to collapse into a heap when Zack declared, "I hope it snows really hard and the bus gets stuck and they have to spend the night here with us!" That was one time I was so grateful his prayers were NOT answered!

Zack was like me in many ways, one being he had a heart for others, especially those who were hurting or in need. One of my favorite photos is of him kneeling on the floor, taping gift wrap around one of his favorite lightsabers. He'd decided that since the kids I serve in Ghana didn't have any toys, he was going to give them his. Instead of selecting the things he didn't like or had grown tired of, he picked out his favorite toys and wrapped them up for me to take on my next trip. I tried to reason with him that he might regret that decision in the future, and he admonished me for being selfish. He said, "If I give them things I don't really like, then they probably won't really like them either." I didn't know how to explain to him that kids who had escaped a civil war in Africa had never seen *Star Wars* and had no clue what a lightsaber was, or that Buzz Lightyear wasn't a character they were familiar with. I just smiled at his generous heart and took them on my next trip.

These are the memories I cherish most when I shut my eyes and try to hear his voice in my head. My young child giving away his favorite toys to kids in a refugee camp ten thousand miles away. Zack sneaking two loaves of my fresh-baked banana bread out of the house and up the hill to his best friend Michael's house to share with his family. Zack inviting a crowd big enough to fill an auditorium to our house for lunch, knowing I would do whatever necessary to accommodate them. Zack bringing a teenage girl home from school, asking if she could stay because her addicted mother had lost their apartment and the girl was sleeping in a car...

He brought at least ten or twelve friends home at different times, pulled me into my room and shared in confidence that they were hungry, homeless, had been beaten, or were addicted to something and he needed me to talk to them. He even asked me to go visit with the custodial grandparents of one girl, insisting that they needed help because the girl had health issues that were going untreated.

It's hard sometimes to remember the timber of his deep voice, so I call his cell number just to hear his recorded message. And then I cry. Usually until my face is swollen and my stomach is churning. I ugly cry. I haven't made it through a single day yet that I haven't had at least one breakdown, but I try to go crazy in the privacy of my own room away from my youngest children who are still at home. Late at night, when my show is over, when the house is quiet and the kids are all asleep is the hardest time of all. Zack was a night owl and he would wait for me to finish the show, then he would bounce down the stairs and meet me in the kitchen with a huge grin and a proposal, like "How would YOU like to make ME some nachos?" He'd deliver the lines like a game show host giving you an opportunity to win ten thousand dollars. His huge silly grin would always melt my heart, even though he drove my husband Paul crazy with the ease with which he manipulated me. Paul would snap, "He should have eaten dinner with the rest of us. You shouldn't cook him extra food, let him eat leftovers." But I dismissed his complaints and made Zack whatever his heart desired. He really wasn't hard to please, his tastes were simple but specific. He wanted Dinty Moore beef stew, Nally's chili, and homemade tacos or nachos. When he was younger he wanted tuna fish sandwiches on white bread with mayo. Nothing else. Plain, simple, no spice.

After his funeral, a friend named Stephen came by the house and asked to talk with me. He was a big kid and seemed awkward in his own skin. He asked if he could share something with me, and began to shake as he choked out his words.

He said: "A few years ago my folks went through a divorce, my dad left and Mom was trying to keep us together. She was broke, so I couldn't afford lunch. I was sitting in the cafeteria all alone, and Zack saw me. I'm not cool like he was, but he came over to my table and asked 'How's it going? Why aren't you eating?' I shrugged my shoulders and told him that I didn't have money for lunch. He smiled and disappeared. A few minutes later he came back with an entire plate full of food for me. When I told him I couldn't pay him he said, 'don't worry, my mom won't mind.'"

Stephen went on to say that Zack didn't just bring him lunch, he sat with him as he ate, and talked to him. He said that every day for weeks Zack bought him lunch and sat and ate with him. After a few days, Zack's other friends stopped by and joined them and after a few weeks, he no longer felt like he was the odd kid without any friends. By this time, he was crying, and so was I. "Zack probably saved my life that year," he said. "I was so depressed. I can't believe he didn't know how much everyone loved him."

The thing is, Zack *did* know everyone loved him. He knew he was loved by his family and friends, he knew that he was the apple of his father's eye and that he had me wrapped around his little finger. His depression wasn't for lack of love, he became depressed because of circumstances that were difficult and troubling. A storm that lead to a car accident that caused him to fear driving. A move to a different town to be with his father. A new school. A breakup with a girl. An illness that caused him to miss school and led to him not graduating on time. All these things added up to a bout with depression that stole his joy and his huge smile. His dad and I got him to a counselor who got him to a doctor, who advised him to go on antidepressants. I had no clue, nor did his father, how fatal a decision that would prove to be.

Within a few weeks of beginning the medicine, Zack stopped being the boy I gave birth to—the child I had raised. Gone was the young man on the autistic spectrum who could not stand for a piece of garbage to remain in his garbage can overnight. Gone was the boy whose room was spotless and every single stuffed animal was in its assigned space. Gone was the kid who loved to sing and skateboard and hang out with friends. In his place was someone I did not know. This new Zack was angry all the time, snapping at me and his siblings. He had moved back home from his dad's, his room became a pigsty, and he wouldn't even put his clothes away. Zack was always, always, always the neatest, cleanest child in the family. That ended, and his garbage can started to fill with trash and spill over onto the hardwood floors. Piles of clean and dirty clothes mixed on his bed.

When a child is over the age of eighteen, regardless of their emotional age, who drives them to the clinic, or who pays their bills, parents are not consulted about medical treatments. Calls I made about how Zack had started talking about déjà vu and time travel went unreturned. Later, I found out that in response, his medication had been *INCREASED.*

I thought the medication would help him, and that antidepressants were just that, medicine to combat depression. I had no clue how deadly the poison that was given to my beautiful son was. No idea when I asked him "did you take your medicine today?" that I was contributing not to his mental wellbeing, but to his demise.

Without telling me or his dad, he decided on his own that the side-effects of the drugs were too much for him to handle, and he quit taking his medication. The only people he told were young friends who did not know how deadly a decision that would be, and did not know to tell us. On Tuesday, September 26, he asked me to help him figure out how to apply to Bellevue College so he could take filmmaking classes in the fall of 2018. On Wednesday, September 27, he asked me to make an appointment with our dentist, so he could get braces again; his teeth had shifted, and he didn't want them to continue to get crooked. On Thursday morning, the 28th, the day before I left for my annual trip to Africa, he came into my room before the sun was up. My hubby was in Oregon at the ranch he manages, and Zack tapped on the door as he often did, then came in and picked up Sophia, the schnauzer, put her on my bed and told me to scooch over. He laid down on top of the blankets next to me and pulled my arm up over his shoulder. I played with his beautiful long, curly hair as he pet the dog next to us. I fell back asleep stroking his hair, listening to him breathing, and woke to hear him singing in the shower.

The next day I set my alarm for three a.m. to head to the airport for Africa. I tried to go into his room to say goodbye, but the door was locked. I tapped and told him to open it, he said he was sleeping. I said I was leaving for Ghana and would not see him for two weeks, and he sleepily replied "I'll see you when you get home, love you, Mom" Had I known what he was going to do just four days later I would have broken the door off the hinges with my bare hands, pulled him from his warm bed and held him in my arms for days or weeks or months or however long it would take for his mind to clear and think reasonably once again. But I didn't. I just turned and walked down the stairs and into the car and rode to the airport where I departed for Ghana.

Zack left the farm on his sister Shaylah's birthday, the 29th, and went back to his dad's house. He went to counseling on Friday evening and was upbeat and cheerful during an almost two-hour session. He spent the weekend skateboarding, hanging out with friends, watching *Star Wars*, and enjoying his dad's home-cooked Costa Rican foods. He played video games with his friends and stayed up late on Sunday night laughing. He caught a bus, then the ferry, to get back to the farm on Monday, frustrating his tutor because he missed classes Monday morning (she wrote to me in Ghana complaining that he was not in school). I sent him a text and called Paul, leaving him a message to talk to Zack to remind him he couldn't miss school if he was going to catch up and graduate.

He got a ride from the ferry dock to the house from a friend, who spent time with him in the barn playing with four kittens a friend had rescued and brought to us. He came in the house, talked to his siblings, and ate dinner with the family. After dinner, he went up to his bedroom and closed the door. A few hours later he headed downstairs with his coat on and his headphones in. Paul questioned him and he said he was going for a walk to clear his head, that he was stressed. Paul argued with him but let him go, figuring he was going to go smoke pot, something he and his friends had been doing the past year.

A short time later Zack sent Paul a text message telling him he was sorry for being argumentative, and that Paul should not wait up for him, he would be gone a while. Paul figured he was up the hill at Michael's house and went to bed. When he didn't hear him come in, he sent him a text at 1:30, asking him if he had made it in. The next day his room was empty, and Paul assumed he had caught the 6:50 bus for school and went about his day. It wasn't until I was contacted in Africa to say that Zack had missed another day of school that we began to panic, but it was already too late.

He had left a note in his room, under his pillow. A two-page rambling letter talking about time travel, déjà vu, how he had to reset the "time continuum" and this was the only way to do it. He said he was sorry if he hurt us, but he thought he would wake up in his own bed the next day and have to do it all over again until "he got it right." He wrote that time is like a river with bends and curves and he could step in and out at any point, and that he had been doing it for centuries. All delusional images created in his young brain by the SSRIs he had taken, and then discontinued.

The medicine he was on should never be given to young people. Blind study drug tests have proven it causes delusions and suicidal or homicidal thoughts in almost half of the young people who take it. And yet it is legal, and the only requirement is that the makers put a "black box warning" on the first prescription, stating it can be deadly, must be taken under supervision, and should not be discontinued. A black box warning that I never saw, his father never saw, and was never explained to either one of us. It was the local coroner who made a comment that made me wonder what he was talking about. He said, "This is the third teenage suicide I have dealt with in the last few weeks, all of them were on the same prescription drug."

The nightmare that was my life got even more hellish as I delved into thousands of pages of reports and studies that show how deadly SSRIs are, especially for people under the age of twenty-five. The initial report given to the FDA shows that the drugs are no more effective at combating depression than a placebo, and yet they can cause delusions and increase suicidal ideology in more than 45 percent of young people given the medicine. *NO MORE EFFECTIVE THAN A PLACEBO?* I spent the next three months in a stupor of blind rage waiting for the toxicology reports to come back, and when they did I was shaken once again. He had nothing in his system. No weed. No alcohol. No drugs that would cause him to be delusional like LSD or meth. Nothing.

Mike Allen, his choir director wrote me this note shortly after Zack left us:

I've struggled to put my thoughts into words. Zach was one of the most unique kids I've ever known. He was strangely confident yet needing reassurance all the time. He came to me as a creative and excited kid with some limited skills but a ton of energy and excitement. He wanted so badly to be a part of the groups and quickly became a class favorite! He was loved by everyone for sure. One of the best things about Zach is that he was an encourager and helper to anyone. At times it was almost annoying because even when he wasn't one hundred percent on his

OWN music, he was offering to help others. Man, that's a heart of gold! He would literally move next to people that were struggling and encourage them.

Zach was excited about rehearsals but he was a different kid when he was performing. There was a joy about him that came on as soon as he was on stage. Madrigal Feaste was clearly his thing. Costumes, stories, serving, acting... did I mention costumes? He loved it.

I saw Zach the week before school started. He was showing someone around the school. I didn't see him at first but he yelled down the hall at me... "Hey, Mr. Allen! How's it going?" I turned around and he proceeds to introduce me as the "best teacher at SK." Man, I didn't think much about it at that point. It was just Zach's encouraging spirit trying to lift ME up. What a gem.

I knew very little about Zach's struggles. I wish I had known more. I wish I could have helped and been more available to him. I regret not taking more time to know his struggles.

I learned from Zach. I learned to be more encouraging. I learned to not take life for granted. I learned to not take my students for granted. I want to get to know my students more because of Zach. I value those kids that aren't the "traditional" kids. They can have an outlet in choir, as well as find a home in a school that is so big that kids can feel lost. I'm more focused on reaching those kids now.

I cannot imagine your pain, but I also see your faith on display for the world to see. There is no way to ease the pain but knowing that Zach is in the arms of Jesus is a start. God works ALL THINGS together for good for those that love Him. Who knows what good is coming from this, but God's promises are true.

Blessings,
Mike Allen.

Zachariah Miguel Rene-Ortega was a challenging, wild, passionate, talented, charming, manipulative, defiant boy. Filled with compassion for the outcast and a wicked sense of humor, he was my most challenging child in many ways, but also the apple of my eye.

While the pain is even worse than the pain I had when he came into this world, it is oddly the same. Only instead of my body tearing and bleeding, it is my heart.

I wrote this poem the day after I landed and went to the funeral home to see my once vibrant son:

In violence he was born, a rush of bloody fluids that exploded into the room only a minute after I arrived... and in violence he departs. I prayed with all my being at his arrival, grey and small and lifeless as he entered. The only sign of life were his big open eyes, looking beyond me to something I could not see.

And as I screamed for the doctors to revive him on the birthing table, they got oxygen to his tiny frame and in time the grey skin was replaced by pink, and the breaths came on his own. This time I was not there to scream for the doctors to revive him, the oxygen was long gone from his lungs by the time his wiry frame was freed from the rope.

I know not how to think or feel, so I cling to God in my darkest hour and find peace in knowing I loved my son fiercely. I am convinced only the Lord in Heaven loved him more. I pray that God forgave him his youthful foolishness as easily as I did and overlooked his character flaws. He will not be in my arms again until my name is called, but I pray the Lord is holding him and telling him that he is loved in such a way that I could not.

I loved you with every fiber of my being Zachariah, and I will love you for all eternity son. Rest in the arms of our Lord and I pray you have found the peace in death that you could not find in life.

I won't hold my last born biological baby again until eternity. I won't stroke his long, beautiful hair, or feel his breath against my skin. I won't hear his voice—except for the few recordings I have—until I see Jesus face to face. I hope the Lord won't mind if I rush to hold both Zack and his older brother Sammy in my arms before getting the tour of paradise.

When Zachariah left us, I know that his older brother, Sammy, was waiting at heaven's gate with a wide smile.

Sammy Young D'zolali Rene was a part of our family for just two years before God called him home on March 11, 2013. I had adopted Sammy from an orphanage in Ghana, West Africa, and he instantly became a part of our extended family and a huge part of our hearts.

Sammy's love and happiness were infectious; his broad smile would light up the room. All who met him were touched by his silly, fun personality and his unconditional love. Sammy was born in Ghana; we know not when, we know not where, we know not who bore him. When he was a toddler, he was found wandering the streets of a village, lonely, hungry, and cold. Schoolchildren took him in and fed him scraps from their lunches and allowed him to sleep in the schoolroom at night. They named him D'zolali, meaning "spirits fly"...

After a time, the school's headmistress tried to locate family members, and no one claimed him, so Sammy was taken to Osu Children's Home, an orphanage in the capital city of Accra, and there he stayed. An auntie was eventually located and told the director of the orphanage that Sammy would scream at night and writhe on the floor. They believed he was possessed by demons, and they tried to cast the evil spirits out. Then they would beat him. When that didn't stop his screaming, they put him out in the street to die. Little did they know he was writhing in pain because of sickle cell anemia, a genetic blood disorder that afflicts many in West Africa.

Sammy spent most of his life in Osu without ever having a single visitor or a relative come to see him. He never received a Christmas present, never had a birthday celebration. He never had his own room; he never learned how to read or write. He was often cold and hungry; there was never enough food for the kids at the home. He never had new soccer shoes or his own soccer ball, but he did have the talent to draw, so he would sit for hours and draw pictures for the other children living in the home. When visitors would come to see the other kids, Sammy would hurriedly draw a picture to bless them.

When he had his sickle cell attacks, he would be told by the aunties running the home to be quiet and to go lie down, because he was disturbing the other children. Eventually, a sweet lady named Auntie Annie came to the home and took an interest in Sammy. She would carry him to the street, get him on a crowded bus and take him to the hospital, where he would be given something to ease his excruciating pain.

In 2010, while working in Ghana, I went to Osu and met Sammy. He had been very sick the day I was there and stayed at the orphanage instead of going to school. He was sitting at a small table in the sun, drawing pictures for the other children in the home who didn't attend school. When I met him, he gave me the picture he was drawing and put his name on it. I took his small, stubby pencil and drew a picture of him, and handed it to him as a gift. As the Lord would have it, there was another lady at the orphanage that day, Laurie Thibert, who lives in the Puget Sound area. Laurie was adopting a boy from the orphanage, Osei, and she knew Sammy well. She offered to help me to keep in touch with Sammy by sharing the cell phone she had left at the orphanage for her son, Osei. I knew in my heart that Sammy was special, talented, and lonely, and that I loved him—I just didn't have a clue how special he really was at that time or how much more I would grow to love him.

So it became a pattern. Every Sunday morning Laurie would call me and tell me that she had just spoken to Osei, and Sammy was waiting to talk to me. After a few weeks of wrestling with the Lord and insisting that I could not handle adopting any more children, God had given me peace and the strength and courage I needed. A lawyer was found, and the insane paper trail began. It took a full year to complete the adoption and obtain Sammy's visa to come to the US.

During that time I took him out of Osu and put him in a foster home situation at Buduburam, the refugee camp my NGO, Point Hope, works in. In no time at all, Sammy had all the employees of Point Hope and probably half the residents of the camp wrapped around his little finger. His charm and warmth touched all he met. He had his first real family in Buduburam. He lived with a young man named TC and then moved in with Kwasie and Aunt Essie...he was so loved and cherished, and when I came to take him home to America, they did not want to let him go.

Once he was home in America, he could not get enough love and affection. He was like a little puppy, wanting to be held and loved on constantly. He would run his fingers through my hair, sit on my lap, drape his gangly arms around me every chance he got. After a few months, that began to change, and he rapidly matured into a sweet young man, far too mature to be held by this mama bear. He worked hard at everything he put his hand to. He loved having his own room, and he kept it spotless and neat. He loved having several changes of clothes, and his fashion sense was impeccable. His shoes looked as if he had never worn them, because he would clean them every day. He made his bed each morning and put his things away neatly. He got frustrated when his siblings would not help out around the house, and he was constantly telling me to go sit down, he would do whatever task I was working on.

Sammy loved to eat, to laugh, to tease, to draw and paint, and to dance. He had a sense of rhythm like Michael Jackson and moved like he had taken years of dance lessons. He was always the life of the party, and we had many parties in the short time he was a part of our lives. Before each party he would say he wasn't going to attend, that it would be boring, and then he would end up being the center of attention each time!

On the first night he was fully my son, Sammy told me through his tears that he never dreamed God would answer his prayers. He said, "Mama, I always thought I would die alone in the orphanage. That I would never know what it was like to have someone love me." And after several racking sobs, he continued, "And no one would know that I had ever lived."

He died in our arms, he died surrounded by people he loved, and none of us will ever forget that he lived. That he lived life filled with God's grace and mercy. That he lived life filled with hope for the future. That he lived a life that was worthy of God's calling, and that he lives on in our hearts every day going forward.

∽

My son Sammy waited a long time to have a family; I, on the other hand, waited merely minutes for my salamander friend to come back to life. Both were miracles of different magnitudes, yet both left deep impressions upon the hearts of their witnesses.

I knew the salamander and the owl were signs from God that things really could live again, and it fueled my codependent adolescent spirit to pray harder, to try harder, to bring life to souls that appeared to be long gone. And well into adulthood, I've seen Him bring people back to life who didn't necessarily lack a heartbeat, but did lack the heart to go on. I have prayed into the lives of friends and family who've lost themselves somewhere along the way, and many times over I've seen a revival of spirit, purpose, and love where hopelessness had once settled in.

Sammy prayed this type of restoration into his own story, that he would be loved, that he would not die alone, and that his very existence would be recognized by *anyone*—and in fact his story has touched *thousands*.

Zack prayed this type of restoration into the many outcasts, loners, and all those kids like himself, different from their peers, whom he instinctively knew were in need of his generous heart. Just as he had prayed it into the kids from the African Children's Choir, and in doing so, he prayed them into our lives.

In the days and weeks after I lost my boys, I was one of those who did not know if I had the heart to go on. When Zack took his own life, I had to step away from my radio program for three weeks before I could find the strength and courage to put my voice back on the air. The outpouring of love, support, and prayer from my listeners—the hundreds of thousands of you who in that moment stopped to considered where *my* heart was—restored me.

Zack and Sammy's purposes far surpassed the end of their lives here on Earth. Their stories will continue to be told in hopes that people like you who read this book will understand that God has a vision for your life, a purpose to pray for, and miracles in store for you along the way.

Yes, miracles of very different magnitudes... but wouldn't you know... the tiny salamander who lived before my five-year-old eyes planted a seed of faith in things unseen, which grew and rooted into a deep belief that my sons, Zack and Sammy, who died, still live.

CHAPTER 2:
A HEART BECKONED

S itting in my cramped studio built beneath a stairwell
in an old brick building that stood next to the mono-
rail tracks in Seattle, Washington, I was two hours into
my nightly five-hour broadcast, scrolling through my in-
box and answering my request lines.

Delete, delete, delete... stop and read, delete, answer, delete, read live on the air, went the cadence of my
computer use in between "Hi, you've reached the *Delilah*
show. Who's with me on the phone lines?" On this particular December night, I started to hit delete on one
of a dozen scam letters I had gotten. They usually begin, "Dear sir or madam, you are receiving this because I
was given your name by a colleague..." And usually end
with, "If you kindly give me your name, Social Security

number and routing address I will gladly deposit ten million dollars into your account. You must not tell anyone about our arrangement..."

But before my right hand instinctively hit delete, I paused and kept reading.

> *Dear Madam,*
>
> *My name is Winifred Ticley.*
>
> *I understand you adopt black children. I am wondering if you would consider adopting my three children. They are starving. We have no food or fresh water. We living in a refugee camp called Buduburam in Ghana, West Africa. If you cannot, may God bless you anyway.*
>
> *Sincerely, Winifred Ticley*

I stopped. Read it again. Shook my head at how absurd this communication was, and then instead of delete, I hit reply.

"Who are you and how did you know I have adopted children? How did you get my email address?"

At that point I was a single mom with a family of seven, three biological children and four adopted, ranging in age from twenty down to two.

Several hours later, before leaving my studios for the night, I got a reply. "I am Winifred Ticley. A mother of three. There is an Internet café near to the refugee camp where we live. I was in a Christian chat room begging for support for my children and someone said that a white lady named Delilah is famous and has adopted black children. Would you adopt mine?"

Back and forth we wrote over the next few days—someone claiming to be a Liberian refugee named Winifred Ticley, and me. I googled Buduburam and found a few mentions of it on the Internet; it was indeed a refugee camp in Ghana. I googled information about the Liberian population living there and read about the horrific civil wars that had ravaged this tiny West African nation for over two decades, leaving almost a million dead and another half million displaced in refugee camps and neighboring countries. I read about the videotaped executions, massacres, tortures, blood diamonds, rice taxes, and crowded, festering refugee camps. I read about cholera, HIV, starvation, malaria, and the UNHCR. The more I read, the more I was convinced that this was some sort of bizarre hoax, but why? And why me?

By the third day, after a dozen or so email exchanges, I was going nuts. The part of me that always rushes to rescue or help was bridled by the absurdity of the situation and the enormity of the requests—adopt my starving children? But what if they really were starving? Winifred suggested I wire her money, adding to my suspicion that this was somehow a huge hoax.

On night four after the first email, I went to bed and slept fitfully between my two wiggling boys, Zack, three, and Thomas, two, who always found their way into my room by two a.m. At about four a.m. I sat up straight in my bed, wide-awake, with the name Richard Stearns impressed upon my heart. "Richard Stearns?" I said it out loud, trying to remember where I had heard that name, and who he was. I padded out to my makeshift home office and typed in Richard Stearns... oh yes, he was the president of World Vision, one of the world's largest and most respected NGOs. I had met him on an earlier occasion and had even lent my voice to their on-hold recordings for their organization.

Dear Richard, I typed... and began to explain my fascinating but troubling conversation with the supposed Winifred Ticley. I forwarded our email dialogue and asked him if there was any way World Vision could investigate if the claims were true, if Winifred was a real person, if she had starving children, and finally if I could give a grant to World Vision to care for them. Satisfied, I went back to bed and slept peacefully for the next few hours.

At about eight thirty, my phone rang and a rich, smooth, warm voice greeted me. "Good morning, Delilah, this is Rich Stearns. You are not going to believe this, but standing in my office right now is a man who helped to establish the refugee camp Buduburam many years ago. It was such a coincidence that I received your email this morning, since I had scheduled a meeting with this man."

This man meeting with Richard had worked in Buduburam for World Vision when the camp was first established. He also lived and worked in Liberia after the civil war was over, trying to help people put their lives back together. And although he had not been to the refugee camp in several years, I was told he could help me locate Winifred Ticley.

Rich Stearns proceeded to invite me to the World Vision offices, which were only about forty minutes south of my home. What were the chances of somebody being in an office forty minutes away who had actually worked and lived in this supposed refugee camp over ten thousand miles away? My car wasn't the only thing racing down Interstate 5 as I headed to the meeting, my mind was going a hundred miles an hour!

At World Vision, I was ushered into a conference room, where I was joined by half a dozen people, including the eloquent Dr. Joseph Riverson. Rich introduced himself and then Dr. Joe, a very dark-skinned man with a huge smile and a voice like velvet. His deep baritone sounded like music, even with a simple "hell-ow." Dr. Joe was born and raised in Ghana, where the queen's English is the national language, then studied medicine in Ireland, and he has lived in dozens of countries around the world while working for World Vision.

I was astonished at how naturally the conversation flowed. It was as if I was standing outside of my own body observing the miracle swirling around me. I was speechless at first, unable to conceive how just a week or two prior to this meeting, I'd never given Ghana (or any part of West Africa) a second thought. How I had never thought about people living in refugee camps or what their living conditions might be. How I had never heard of this little 128-acre patch of red clay soil called Buduburam, and now I was seated with a man who had once lived and worked in this obscure refugee camp. And it was all brought to my attention through a strange email I nearly deleted.

I sat quietly listening to World Vision team members tell me about their presence in Ghana. They showed me photos of the country and graphs illustrating how many children were malnourished or starving. Dr. Joe spoke of his years working in the camp and how he helped to install massive poly tanks to store fresh water, but how the system had fallen into disrepair and been abandoned. World Vision found it impossible to carry out their model for sustainability in a camp with a transient population and so many foreign and domestic governments trying to run it, so they had withdrawn their field officers many years prior.

But yes, they could tell me there was a woman named Winifred Ticley living in the camp and yes, she was caring for children who were actually her younger siblings. The family had fled on foot when their small village in Liberia was attacked and their mother was killed. Winifred had carried the youngest child on her back and urged the other two to walk as they trudged across several hundred miles to safety.

I asked if I could present a check to World Vision to be used to purchase food, water, clothes, and mattresses as well as pay rent on a small apartment for Winifred and the children. They agreed to facilitate the process of helping this little family unit stay together, and I stood up to go feeling very accomplished and satisfied with my efforts. As I was leaving, a tall, thin man named David Snow said, "Great, you have just helped save the lives of four people in the refugee camp. What do you intend to do for the eighty thousand others who are dying?"

I smiled and (in retrospect) smugly replied, "They didn't write to me; they aren't my problem."

I walked a few steps out the door toward my beat-up old van when I felt God's wrath fall upon me so hard I literally crumpled to my knees crying. I turned and rushed back in to catch the team before they had dispersed. Most were still in the doorway gathering their computers and water bottles, when I wiped my tears and apologized for my offhand comment. "I am so sorry," I managed to choke out. "But I'm just one person. What can I do?"

I didn't have a passport. I'd never been anywhere outside the United States except for a few trips to Mexico and Canada. That was the extent of my worldly travels. No long weekends in the South of France, no strolls along the Thames, no trips to Ireland to see the lush green fields and flocks of snowy-white sheep, though when I dreamed of travel, this had been my vision.

I'd spent all of my adult life working at various radio stations around the country and raising children. When I did allow myself to fantasize about world travels, it certainly wasn't to visit a refugee camp in impoverished West Africa. In fact, the notion had never entered my mind.

I stepped out of the little wood shack my father had built for the kids in the neighborhood to protect us from the damp Oregon rain as we waited for the school bus. The bus shack was at the end of a long gravel road, beneath the abutments of a bridge that crossed over the Coos River. Our home, a hundred-plus-year-old farmhouse, was about a mile away at the end of Lillian Slough (pronounced *slew*), a finger of tidal water once used to store logs before they were floated to the mill that sat just to the north of the bridge.

My straight blond hair hung down my back and I proudly wore a beautiful new coat my mother had made for me. I'd just turned seven years old and was in second grade. We were dirt poor, but I never knew it at the time. I was completely oblivious to the financial struggles my parents faced on a daily basis.

My dad Richard, known as Dick, worked hard to provide for his small family. I had an older brother, Matthew, a younger sister, DeAnna, and Mom was pregnant with the fourth, Timothy, who came along in the fall of that year.

On this particular cold, wet day, I was feeling quite lovely wearing my new coat. My mother's old sewing machine was set up in the cheery kitchen of the farmhouse we rented. It was the original homestead on an eighty-acre milk-cow farm that was owned by a family named Mikulecky whose parents had immigrated from Bohemia (the present-day Czech Republic). Each night after dinner, Mom sat at her sewing machine, a cup of black coffee and a Pall Mall Gold cigarette burning close by.

Mom was a fabulous seamstress. People would bring her old clothes, shirts, dresses, even blankets and table-cloths, and she would tear them apart, stitch them back up on her old machine, add buttons and lace, and create something entirely new. The coat I was wearing that day had been refashioned from one my grandma gave her. She took it apart, repurposed it, and created a gorgeous green winter coat with a black hood made of soft velveteen. It kept my hair dry and felt gentle on my skin.

I jumped across the mud puddles, trying not to get any mud on my new coat. Jumping was not easy for me; I had braces on my legs, the same kind Forrest Gump wore when he ran down the driveway. (I cried when I watched that movie, remembering how awkward, ugly, and out of place I always felt wearing my braces.) But on this particular day, the happiness from the pretty new coat outweighed the contraptions my legs were bound in, known as "clod-hoppers" to my classmates.

I climbed on the bus and took my usual seat. My brother, Matt, pushed past me to sit with the kids who lived up the slough from us, and I sat down next to the windows toward the front. At the next stop, a girl named Kathy got on and sat next to me. Her shoulder-length curly blond hair was damp, and short bangs stuck to her forehead. She was a pretty girl with wide-set eyes and a broad smile. The plaid dress she wore was also wet, and she only had a thin sweater on to fend off the damp Oregon chill. My cheerful mood about my own new coat was lost in the moment as she sat next to me, her teeth chattering as she tried to get warm. Every time we stopped to pick up more kids, the clunky door let in the cold wind and she'd shiver again...

That night over dinner I begged my mom to make a coat for Kathy. I told her I'd give Kathy my new coat if she'd let me and I'd wear my old, tight one. Mom insisted I sit up and eat my dinner and not worry about Kathy's problems.

The next day I "slipped" while jumping over a mud puddle and fell in. It wasn't hard to imagine, given the clumsy braces, and I ended up a muddy, soaking-wet mess. I *may* have purposely missed the bus... Mom didn't have a car to drive me to school, so she had to ask our neighbors—whom we called Ma and Pa Fry—if they would take me. I begged her to come with me and told

Delilah

her she'd need to talk to my teacher in order to excuse my tardiness. She relented and came with me to school.

Lucky for me, the timing was perfect; we arrived just minutes after the bus. I ran to join my class, lining up in front of the school, pulling my mom's hand to stand by us. Each week we had a new line leader, and then as the flag was raised we said the pledge of allegiance. Rain or shine, we did this every day before entering the building. Kathy was directly in front of me, and like the day before, she stood shivering in the morning mist in a thin cotton blouse and a worn navy-blue cardigan that was much too small.

That night Mom sat at her machine, and the next day she handed me a brown paper bag. "Give this to Kathy and tell her if it's okay with her mom, she can have it, that it's an extra coat since you just got a new one." I didn't dare open it or even peek; she had folded the top of the bag and put a single staple in the middle.

When Kathy climbed on the bus, she smiled and sat down by me. Her curly hair was uncombed, her saddle shoes were scuffed, and she had on the same threadbare navy-blue cardigan. I couldn't hold back my excitement as I thrust the bag at her. "My mom said if your mom says it's okay, you can have this coat. It's an extra."

She took the staple out and pulled the coat from the bag. Mom had refashioned a man's navy dress coat—an actual navy uniform top with the wide collar and white stripes—into a stunning coat for my friend. For a moment I was jealous—with her curls and her new coat, she looked like Shirley Temple! But I was so happy when I saw how proud she was of her new coat that my jealousy faded into sheer joy!

Looking back, I suspect my mom stayed up all night to cut, line, and sew that coat. She never mentioned it again, except to tell Kathy how nice she looked when she saw her at the next school affair. Kathy never knew my mom had created the coat just for her. And I don't ever remember seeing her mom at any of our community gatherings. Many times in the future, my mother would purse her lips and snap at me, "Mind your own business, Sis," when I wanted to help someone out, but on this one occasion she came through with flying colors.

∽

Whether it's the hesitation to delete an email from a stranger who lives ten thousand miles away, or the tug at your heart to clothe a neighbor with a warm coat, God will produce great results when you follow through with His divine promptings. I almost walked out of that World Vision meeting and never looked back. Instead, I've since traveled to the Buduburam refugee camp in Ghana dozens of times over a decade. The organization I founded, Point Hope, has installed water tanks that send clean water to spigots throughout the camp. We have career programs for adults, schools for kids, medical stations, farming programs, and we are providing a real, sustainable future for the people I've grown to know and love there.

And to think, I almost didn't hit reply to Winifred's email for help.

To the same tune, my mother didn't want to sew a coat for my friend Kathy, because it's easy to ignore a need when it's not in front of you. But God lined up the events in order to soften her heart and gave her the materials to make the perfect coat for my friend. Who knows how that kind of warmth may have helped Kathy—perhaps to stay focused at school and feel more confident? Maybe it instilled compassion and the desire to help others in need. We rarely ever see the full spectrum of God's plan, and how our simple deeds can spiral into much bigger blessings. Which is exactly why we should consider each good deed an act of God's love and a part of His great plan.

CHAPTER 3:
A DETERMINED HEART

A dirty right foot was balanced atop her left. Skinny legs and arms stuck out from her shorts and T-shirt as a cherubic three-year-old stood at the front gate of the refugee camp, waiting for her mother. Huge dark eyes dominated her dusty brown face framed with short, twisted dreadlocks. She looked past my eyes into my heart, and like most of the hungry children at the refugee camp, she ran straight to me and asked to be picked up.

She was light as a feather and as hard as a rock when I lifted her sixteen-pound frame into my ample white arms. Her body was emaciated from malnourishment, and yet she had the muscles of an athlete. Later, I discovered it was her job to care for her baby sister and to carry water in a bucket perched on her head for the household to use. Not a simple task, as the only freshwater source was almost a three-mile hike, and let's not forget, this child was not far removed from being a baby herself.

I met her on my seventh trip to Ghana. I had the purpose in my heart when I started working in Buduburam, in 2004, to help the community as a whole, not to focus on one or two individuals. I had also decided before I embarked upon starting Point Hope that I was done raising others' children. I was single at the time, had four kids grown and on their own (sort of), and three to go. Almost all of my children have some special needs, either serious health or developmental issues. So adopting more children was not even in my realm of thinking at the time. Until I met Willette...

She had a smile that melted my heart and was incredibly intelligent. In Ghana people carry young children on their backs with the aid of a piece of cotton fabric called a *lappa*. Willette was a bit too old for the lappa and was more content to ride on my hip, her spindly limbs wrapped around my neck and waist. I spent the entirety of that first day with her. She was either attached to me or she was in the arms of my traveling companion, boss, and friend, Kraig. I had sick babies in a lappa on my back and a delightful imp riding on my hip as he and I ferried weak kids back and forth to clinics and doctors that I sponsored in the refugee camp.

We went to a library that Kraig's thirteen-year-old daughter, Erica, had collected over thirteen hundred books to fill—the first public library in a refugee camp in the world. We went to the land I had purchased two years before and saw the organic garden we'd had built—the first sustainable organic farm created to feed the malnourished in a refugee camp. Toward the end of the day, we went to our cramped offices to sit and rest, and the entire time accompanied by this little sprite. When it came time to leave the camp that night, and go back to the hotel room with the other volunteers, I could not peel Willette off me. She screamed and flailed her tiny body when they tried to take her from me. I asked those that I knew in the camp to please go find her mother.

Her birth mother arrived a bit later to fetch her oldest child, and I was shocked at how young she was—barely fifteen when she delivered Willette. I saw that her mom was just a child herself, one who had already given birth twice.

Deconte' was a schoolgirl living in Liberia when a brutal civil war broke out. Most of the people who lived in her small village were killed, violently, with machetes or machine guns. The experience left her nearly catatonic, and she has never really returned to normalcy after living through that hell. Deconte' fled Liberia on foot, along with members of her family, and they made it to the refugee camp in Ghana.

When I met her, she was barely eighteen, with two babies to raise. She reached over to take Willette off my lap, and the child began to scream, refusing to go back to her mother's arms. Deconte' was neither loving nor protective of the live wire in my lap, and after unsuccessfully trying to pull her off, she said, "Keep her" and walked away; it was then I felt the mother Willette had been waiting for could, in fact, be me.

A few days later, one of the security guards at the camp, Rosalee, a strong, light-skinned Liberian woman, asked me if she could introduce me to a child who was in need of some help. She led me to her mud hut, where I met Mercy, a young girl who looked to be about eight. Weighing about fifty-five pounds, she, like Willette, was both spindly and muscular. Her hair was cut close to her head, and her eyes were huge. Rosalee explained that Mercy had been living on the street for some time when she'd taken her in. This child, however, was very strong willed, used to caring for herself, and not inclined to listen to Rosalee's instructions. Understandably, Rosalee was afraid she was going to get hurt.

It took me several years to get the whole story of how Mercy ended up homeless, and suffice to say her young life had been nothing short of horrific. *Tough, tenacious,* and *resourceful* are terms that describe Mercy, because she had to be. She reminded me of a feral kitten, so adorable, but skittish and unable to trust or be tamed.

I spent the week working hard and spending time with both of these little girls who had happened into my life. By the time my plane landed in the US, I knew my resolve to not adopt any more children had melted like the wax used to create the African batik fabric I was wearing. I didn't dare tell anyone, save Kraig, of my decision. He'd seen me cross that emotional bridge when we were working in the muggy heat of Africa, but I was hesitant to tell others. I didn't even share with my best friend (and executive producer of my show) Janey, or my sister, DeAnna, my two confidantes. I was afraid my family or friends might attempt to sabotage my decision.

My younger sons, Zack (bio) and Thomas (adopted), both grew up having pretty intense special needs and required a lot of time and attention. My bio daughter, Shaylah, also has medical issues; she has been medically fragile since birth, with severe asthma and food/environmental allergies. All things considered, adopting any more children, especially those with as much baggage as these two girls had, was pretty crazy. On one level I knew that, but I also knew that God was calling me to be their mother.

In order to adopt Willette and Mercy, I had to have a home study update. And in order to do that, I had to have a case worker come to my house and interview my family members and friends. My assistant, Joni, started asking questions, and when I confided in her that I had planned on adopting two more children, she just laughed out loud, rolled her eyes and said, "Well, what can I do to help?"

I hired a lawyer in West Africa and a lawyer in the US and returned to Ghana to appear before a judge in a sweltering courtroom in a town called Cape Coast. I sat with the two girls, who were busy braiding my sweaty blond hair as we waited for the judge. Thirty minutes later the adoption was completed and papers were signed.

Then the hardest part of the process began—waiting for the United States to grant an entry visa to my girls. This process takes months, so I placed the girls in a foster care situation in Ghana and returned home. I called them as often as I could and sent packages, presents, and pictures of their family in America. Once the adoption had been finalized in Ghana, I told my family and friends. Most were not only supportive, but also a little angry that

Delilah

I had not told them sooner. Prayers were sent up as I flew back to Ghana to work and to visit my girls.

Leaving them at the airport, not knowing when or even if their visas would be approved, was one of the hardest things I have ever done as a mother. Listening to them cry and beg me not to leave was excruciating. No amount of consoling them or bribing with trinkets or sweets made it any less painful. It was sheer hell.

I came home again, prepared my family and my house as best I could, and waited. When the notice finally arrived that their visas had been approved, I packed my bags and took the nineteen-hour trip to Ghana (five to New York, a three-hour layover, then eleven more to Ghana). I landed, collected the girls, and went to stay at a local hotel while we waited for the embassy to give us the visas. One day, two days, three rolled by... I distracted the girls by teaching them how to swim. Neither of them had been in the water before, but despite their lack of experience, they had no fear of it—shallow or deep end. We swam, and they ate copious amounts of food. A buffet at the hotel was an amazing sight and experience for them— something out of a fantasy. Boiled eggs were consumed by the dozen that week. Finally, the visas were ready and we raced to the embassy, got them affixed to their passports, gathered all their documents and adoption papers, and raced to the airport in congested Accra traffic.

We arrived two hours before our plane was to depart, but fifteen minutes past the required check-in time. The ticket agent told us we could not proceed and informed us new tickets must be purchased for the next flight out, which would be in two days. This was unacceptable on all levels, as our plane had not even landed or been cleaned. I placed a frantic call back to the States, which sent Kraig into action and resulted in him reaching a Delta official at three a.m. The Delta official had to call their international office in order to reach the agents in Africa. The girls were crying and scared, the agents were rigid and unmoved, and I was damned determined to get home in time to see my boys, Zack and Thomas, nicknamed TK, play in their opening Little League game. I'd told them I would not miss their first game, and I was going to keep my word! The Accra agent finally relented and released us to run to the gate.

The airport at that time had no escalator or elevator, just endless stairs and ramps. Carrying Willette and holding Mercy's thin hand, we ran to the plane. They boarded us through the back of the jet and seated us, separately, in the last three rows. Willette was two rows ahead of me, Mercy was directly in front of me, and I was against the back wall. I pleaded with those seated near us to switch, but they refused. So I told them the girls had never been on an airplane before and asked them to please comfort them for me if they started crying. Almost on cue, Willette wiggled out of the seat belt and climbed over the seat to be with Mercy, who in turn began to cry and reach for me. I tried to soothe them, but I was wedged between two large, stubborn passengers. After about five or ten minutes of wailing, the flight attendant who had grudgingly allowed us to get onto the plane finally asked the other passengers to move so the girls could sit with me. These were the same passengers that had been given our preassigned seats that placed us in the same row.

The eleven-hour flight to New York was exciting, nerve-racking, cramped, and uncomfortable. Our plane was two hours late, giving us just an hour to collect our bags, go through customs, recheck our luggage, and catch the next flight. I was frazzled and frantic and told a flight attendant with Alaska Airlines that I *had* to make the flight with my newly adopted girls, because I *had* to get to Seattle to see my boys' baseball game. The flight attendant called ahead to the gate and asked them to hold the plane, and then she *ran* through the airport with us, holding our carryons while I held Willette and Mercy ran along beside us.

We made the plane, we made the game, and we made a family.

About a month after settling into our home, my new baby girl sat on the bench at our breakfast nook eating her fourth or fifth egg of the day. I called to her, "Willette..." No response. I was across the kitchen, so I raised my voice a little louder and said it again—"Willette"—this time a bit annoyed that she hadn't responded with her usual sweet "Yes, Mama?" I looked at her darling little face, her full lips in a half smile and her raised eyebrows, and called her name yet a third time. "Willette, why are you not answering me!"

She smiled broadly and declared in her heavy accent, "Willette stayed in Africa. You said I am your blessing, so now I want to be Blessing." And with that, Willette, and all the trauma and pain, the abuse and neglect, the memories of hunger and thirst, remained in Africa, and Blessing was home to stay.

A week or so later, Mercy came to me and asked, "Mommy, may I change my name, too? I like Mercy, but I would like to be Angel Mercy." So when we went before the judge to get their last names changed to mine, their first names were changed as well. They were four and thirteen at the time they started their new lives with their new names in the States, shedding old identities bound to deep wounds.

Fast forward to now. Angel is an adult making her own way in the world. When she arrived at age thirteen, she was placed in a first-grade school curriculum. She graduated high school four years later with her age group. She's gotten a nursing assistant certification and now works with a disabled child. She has purchased her own car, lives in a house rented with friends, and is attending college. She is beautiful, strong, feisty, and passionate about her faith and her plans. She still does not follow directions, which some say only proves that she *is* her mother's daughter!

Blessing is going into seventh grade, is academically gifted, and a talented writer. It would not surprise me if one day she wrote great novels; she has a wild imagination and talks nonstop! Her characters are colorful, silly, and do wondrous things! She is a bowl of laughter and love that spills over our entire family. She is also a fabulous big sister to her younger biological sister, whom I adopted three years ago, Delilah Jr. They are as close as two sisters can be, and unless you knew their circumstances, you would never know they had ever experienced trauma that would make an *NCIS* episode look soft.

⌒〜⌒

Being born with the show-off gene can be a tremendous thing, especially if you are also endowed with the talent gene. Being born with the show-off gene can pro-pel you into fame, fortune, the movies, or the Olympic winner's circle *if* you can dance, sing, dribble a basketball, throw a football, block a soccer ball, turn backflips on a high wire, or write a play that leaves people speechless... Sadly, something happened to my DNA chain, because although I inherited the show-off gene, I seem to lack the talent portion of the DNA strand.

But what I lack in athletic or musical talent, I make up for in the ability to talk a lot. Since I had braces on my legs as a child, I was often taunted. I quickly realized that if I could laugh at myself, it was much harder for others to make fun of me. Only two years into grade school, I would entertain the class the minute the teacher left the room or turned her back to us. My teacher sent note after note home to my parents asking them to please make me be quiet and stop interrupting class. When they failed to find the off switch for my incessant talking, Mrs. Brown took matters into her own hands and found a roll of duct tape. Frustrated with my constant outbursts, she took a piece of duct tape and put it across my mouth. A few min-utes later I had worked the tape loose with my fingers and tongue, and in her anger and frustration, she wrapped a piece completely around the back of my head. My long dirty-blond hair hung almost to my waist and on this par-ticular day was not in ponytails...

If you look at my class picture, you will notice I have a short bowl-cut hairstyle. The tape stuck and had to be cut out at the end of the day. My grandma took me to the beauty school for a three-dollar haircut the following weekend. The result made me, Grandma, and even my mom cry. It did not, however, get me to shut up! I don't re-member anyone telling me this, or giving me a life lesson, but I realized at an early age you can be a victim or you can be victorious! I used my sense of humor and my ability to weave stories together to entertain the classes year after year, and although the teachers grew frustrated with my talking, they rarely sent me to the principal's office.

In junior high, God stepped in and decided to give me a stage on which to use my show-off gene. Our school, W. F. Jewett Middle School, was in a tiny mill commu-nity next to Reedsport. When I attended, the benefac-tors of the school, W. F. Jewett and his family, had left a large sum of money to be used for academic programs. One such program was a recitation contest, and when I was in seventh grade, the judges were brothers, Jerome and Steve Kenegy. I entered all five categories and won four of them.

At one point, those judges approached Mom and said, "Your daughter *really loves to talk*." Mom stammered and, laughing, said, "I know, we've tried everything to get her to be quiet—even duct tape didn't work." I believe it was broad-faced, jovial Steve who said, "No, this is a good thing for radio. We can put her to work!"

The Kenegy brothers and their engineer, Wes Lockhard, made good on their word and let me write and read school news and sports stories. They set up a work-study program that allowed me to go to school half a day, get all my assignments and take my exams, and then go to the radio station in the early afternoon. I learned how to change the typewriter ribbon on the machines and loved the way it smelled on my skin. They would send me home with miles of news stories, and I'd practice in my bedroom at night, trying to sound as much as I could like the news reporters I saw on television.

Barbara Walters was the only female newscaster I had ever seen, and her speech impediment drove me crazy. There were no women to emulate or admire, but I honestly don't recall ever giving that a second thought. Back in the seventies, I wasn't trying to break the glass ceiling or blaze a new trail for women in media; I just loved talking on the radio and would do anything to hang out at the station all day.

Some time later, I was asked to come to the radio station to do school reports. I did so well, I was asked to do some advertising spots. My knowledge and responsibilities built until I was given my own on-air shifts. By the time I was a junior in high school, I was opening and closing the station. (This was back in the day when local stations ruled the airwaves, and they would sign on and off the air with the National Anthem each day.)

At home, my mom and dad both dealt with their demons and frustrations in different, dysfunctional ways. Dad quit working on projects in the garage and instead spent nearly every night at the local halls, playing pool, avoiding his wife. I don't remember him ever being obnoxious, stumbling or slurring his speech, but I do remember that he more often than not had a drink in hand by five thirty.

The older I got, the more controlling Dad got. When I was young, I didn't notice how much of Mom's daily activities he controlled, or how his anger was toxic in our family. By the time I started wearing a bra and tossing my hair to get attention from the neighbor boys, I was fully aware of his rage seething just beneath the surface and his need to control everyone in our family. Mom turned to others to get her emotional needs met, and I became her confidante. The crazier my family got, the more rebellious I became.

The radio station was my shelter in the storm, and even though I didn't have to be there but a few hours a day, I would stay for hours past the end of my shift recording commercials or just watching Wes work on the equipment. I had no desire to drink or get high, so while my seventies-era classmates were skipping school and heading to the beach to smoke weed, I was running in the rain to get to the studio each afternoon. Fights at home were epic, but I knew if I pushed the boundaries too hard, Dad would deny me the right to go to the station; I walked a fine line and tried to keep my mouth shut so I could stay on the air.

For someone who can't keep a secret and was an angry, rebellious teen, I have no idea how I pulled it off. Maybe since I had started sneaking out of my room at night and meeting up with a certain tall, skinny, redheaded boy in our town, I was giving folks plenty of cause to worry about me in other ways, and my family's issues weren't as worthy of the gossip mill as my own rebellious behavior was.

I worked at KDUN all through high school, as well as at a local fish-packing plant one summer and a bakery the next. When I was younger I babysat, mowed lawns, picked ferns, and peeled a bark called chittam in order to earn money. I wanted to be independent, and one thing Mom taught me as a child was in order to have independence and make your own choices, you had to have your own money. Dad insisted I pay room and board while I was at the radio station, and today I'm glad he did that. Even though at the time I lied and cheated and didn't give him the half he required, I was able to save up several thousand dollars *and* learn how to pay my own living expenses at a very early age.

The day I graduated high school I left home, not really by choice, but by my dad packing the new suitcase I had gotten as a gift and putting it on the front porch when I wasn't home at the appointed hour—the stroke of midnight. He wanted to impart a life lesson and teach me to be humble and obedient. Instead I snuck back into the house the next day, took more of my clothes and the old black leather purse hidden beneath the floorboard, and left for the *big* city.

Coos Bay, Oregon, population twelve thousand! KYNG was a rock station there with more listeners and a hip staff of eight young people who smoked a lot of pot and loved to play the Doobie Brothers every hour. While love of radio bound us together, the cigarettes and drugs set us apart. Whether it was my farm girl moral code or just my fear of messing up on air, I wasn't then or ever interested in either. I still have a great prejudice against smokers and have very little tolerance for it, and absolutely zero when done around children. I'd play smokin'-hot music like the Steve Miller Band, Peter Frampton, and Earth, Wind & Fire, who were regulars on our playlist back in those days!

After a short stint in Coos Bay, my big break came when I moved to the city of Eugene with my best friend,

Dee Dee. I walked into KUGN with a résumé and tape. The program director assumed I had already graduated college and didn't even bother to ask my age. My five-ten stature and my deep voice must have given me an edge. After listening to my tape, he told me to come in the next day to sit in with a DJ named Andy Manuel and watch him do his show. I showed up an hour early, met Andy-man, and got to know the control board. About two hours into his show, Andy was changing the huge reels that provided music on the FM station when the reel exploded and cut his hand. He had to go to the hospital for stitches, and I was left in the studio, on the air. I had no idea what I was doing, but somehow managed to fake my way through the show that night. And the next night. By Monday I was working three six-hour shifts and four hours of production work doing commercials each week.

The next three years I went to school in Eugene, worked at two different radio stations, and went on a lot of dates with gorgeous young men. I don't remember much about school, but I remember the experience at the stations and a few of the hot dates. By the time I was twenty-one, I'd already been fired three times; by the time I was thirty I'd been fired eight times. Sometimes it was for good reasons, but mostly because it was the nature of the industry; a station would get sold or a new program director would come in, and they would clean house and fire all the on-air talent.

Today when someone calls my show, depressed or heartbroken because they have been fired, I often say, "When you've been fired twelve times, call me back, because then we're tied." We laugh together, them thinking I'm joking, me because I'm not.

∽

One time a young male program director in Boston called me into his office and showed me a research project the station had commissioned. He opened the report and basically told me that his research showed that women didn't like hearing other women on the radio and I should simply shut up and play the music. He went on to say if I didn't curtail the talking and just play the songs, I'd need to find a new station to broadcast from, and that no one was interested in hearing my stories or the people I chatted with on the phones. When he was finished with his pie charts and closed the pages, I asked if he was done. He smiled an apologetic, patronizing smile and sat back in his chair.

I was angry and incensed. I reached down and pulled a box of tampons from my purse on the floor, took one out and set it on the cover of the report on his desk. With little restraint, I practically spit out, "When you have to get up at four a.m. and drive to a 7-Eleven to buy one of these because you are bleeding to death, you can tell me what women want. Until then, you don't have a clue."

I was born into a family of angry, angry men. I'm not sure how many generations back it goes, but both my dad and my maternal grandfather were bitter and so very angry. And they tried to control the women they loved: first my grandma, then mom, and then me and my sister. (I'm happy to report none of us obeyed very well!) But I realized early in life that it really didn't matter what I said or did—the men in my family were going to demand I change, no matter what. So it only made sense to me to stay true to myself and follow the path that I knew I had to follow.

Once I left home and got away from the controlling men in my family tree, I ended up working for several more. A few program directors and a few general managers tried to control me. I had learned to navigate the waters of control, manipulation, abuse, and anger as a kid, and I wasn't going to let someone else determine how I was going to be myself. One program director even insisted I change my name! "Delilah sounds like a stripper's name," he said. "From now on you are going to be known on the air as Kelli Star!" I kid you not. No matter how many times I've been told no or told what to say or what image to project on or off the air, I've stuck to my guns and followed my dreams to the life that I get to live today. I'm so blessed and grateful to have been born in the country I was born in, where women have rights and freedoms and we get to make choices for ourselves. In some countries I've been in, I would not be allowed to talk on the radio. In a few countries where I traveled on tour with our military, I wouldn't be allowed to have any of the freedoms I enjoy.

When you decide to use your gifts, talents, and skills to change the world, you may encounter some anger, and probably more than one or two people who may try to stop you. No matter what field you're in, no matter what family dynamic you're in, you will encounter folks who want to control and manipulate you. They'll balk when you announce your plans to volunteer. They'll argue when you say you've decided to be a foster parent, and they'll tell you a million reasons you should not open your heart. Should you get a passport and apply for a visa to travel to a developing nation, a multitude of people you know may tell you horrible tales of atrocities and dangers that have happened to those who've ventured out before you! Photos downloaded from the Internet with every imaginable worm, serpent, skin lesion, or crocodile will be presented to you as proof that you are being foolish to travel afar. Horror stories of volunteers contracting malaria, cholera, hepatitis, and traveler's diarrhea will be shared with you at every meal. I suppose they can't help themselves, these well-meaning manipulators. They believe they are sharing their fears out of love for you; some even believe they are acting as agents of God. They feel it is their moral obligation to set you straight and make it obvious that you should not be a bleeding-heart fool who takes risks that could lead to heartache and destruction.

Pay them no mind. Thank them for their concern and assure them that very few volunteers are actually eaten by a python or a crocodile and that you will keep your hands and your feet in the boat when going through piranha-infested water. Be gracious and kind, but be firm in your resolve to use whatever talents and skills you have to reach out and change the world. Sooner or later they will realize you are not going to stop on your fierce approach to unconditional love, and they will accept your plans and let you fly.

I was mostly silent about adopting Willette and Mercy, because I didn't want to hear another person tell me I shouldn't, nor did I want to see one more eye roll. And no matter how many times I've been beaten up by the stigma of being a woman in radio, fired, and told no, I've stuck to my guns and followed my dream. That's how I've ended up where I am today. Hardheadedness, perseverance, luck, and pluck pay off!

In a similar way, I think my daughter Blessing *knew* I was her mother when we first met at the refugee camp, and though she didn't have many words to express it, she had a fierce grip and determination that wouldn't let me go.

So what is it you want to do? Who do you want to be? Maybe it isn't a career-related goal, but a more personal thing you aspire to. Follow that whisper in your heart, because likely that's God planting a purpose you have yet to uncover. And whatever you do, know this: you will come against opposition whenever you align yourself with God's plan, the naysayers and voices of reason to not do something. But if it's your dream and your purpose to do something and you keep a firm grip on it, God will make a way for it...

CHAPTER 4:
AN OBEDIENT HEART

"I'm going back to the camp," I told my business partner, Kraig, on the phone from my hotel room in Ghana.

"No, you're not," he replied from a meeting he was attending with Point Hope board members in Accra. "It's getting late."

I told him that didn't matter. Something was calling me back to Buduburam, and I had to go.

"Why would you consider going back? It's going to be dark soon," he insisted.

"Because God told me to go," I said.

With that he knew there was no arguing—my mind was made up.

I was exhausted from a busy day of tending to sick moms, pregnant teens, starving babies, abandoned orphans, and demanding men in sweltering heat. At the end of the day, I had been sitting by the pool at our hotel, playing with my two newly adopted daughters, Angel and Blessing, when I suddenly felt the urge to go back to camp. No, not an urge—an insistence. Like a nagging feeling that builds and builds, weighing on your heart until you know it is something you have to do.

I jumped up, grabbed the girls, and headed back to our room to dress and let Kraig know.

Every time I go to Ghana, I try to bring others with me. This trip, I was with my girlfriend Debbie Sundberg and her husband, Brian, who were friends of mine from my rural community in Washington. Brian was a landscape architect who had come to Ghana to help with our organic gardens, and Debbie was a fabulous seamstress who was teaching women job skills that would keep them from having to walk the streets for money.

When I got off the phone with Kraig, I told Debbie I was leaving and asked if she would watch the children. "I'm going with you," she said, so we left my two young, newly adopted daughters with Brian.

There was good reason for Kraig to be concerned for our well-being... Ghana is near the equator. When it gets dark, it gets dark almost instantly. It goes from being absolutely sunny and bright to total darkness in a matter of minutes. And as quickly as the blue-black darkness descends upon West Africa, so does the mood in the camp.

While I never felt unsafe walking around the 128 acres that made up Buduburam during the day, at night

Delilah

it was a completely different environment. Gone were the faces of the teenage mothers I knew and recognized, and the babies I fed and cared for during the day were now all sleeping on straw mats strewn about the floors of mud huts and cinder-block shacks. At night, the camp was pitch-dark, but it came alive with a pulsing, throbbing, demanding energy as throngs of teenagers hung out and danced and laughed in the shadows. It was easy to see why the average birthing age in the camp was only fifteen. The cacophony of the sound was deafening. People shouting to be heard in two or three African languages over distorted native music infused with the odd mix of Kenny Rogers, Madonna, James Taylor, and Lionel Richie. Generally, when the *obruni*—white woman—approached, they quieted down, but once I traveled on a few steps, they went back to talking among themselves in their native tongues and dancing to music that blared over speakers that had been blown out years before.

It really wasn't the dancing, shouting teenagers, nor the drunken brawls that Kraig was worried about, though. His concern was over the bodies that had been found a few days earlier, stabbed and quartered and left on people's doorsteps. Witchcraft, juju, spells, and human sacrifices were usually only spoken about in whispers and hushed tones but sometimes made it into the local newspaper.

Swallowing any fear, Debbie and I found a taxi and bounced along the rutted red roads to the camp. The ride was jarring and rough, and I'm prone to car sickness. Thankfully I managed to make it without throwing up.

Two of my security guard friends at the front gate rushed to meet us. They were frantic.

"We knew you would come back, Mama Delilah!" Beyan exclaimed.

"How did you know I was coming back? I didn't call anyone."

"Because," Beyan replied, "we prayed. We prayed you would come back and now you have."

From a dusty, overcrowded, throbbing refugee camp, a request had been sent into the universe, and back at a comfortable hotel, my heart had heard. My heart had heard it so loudly I could not shut my ears nor refuse the urging in my spirit!

"Why? Why did you pray?"

The men hurried into a nearby hut and brought out a tiny, limp baby. He was so small, maybe ten or twelve pounds, and he fit in Beyan's hands like a naked rag doll. His head was flopped back, and his eyes were glazed over. He looked like he was dead.

They tried to hand the lifeless baby to me, and I startled.

"This is the son of one of the guards," Fidel explained. "The mother is sick. She has a tumor in her stomach and her milk dried up, and no one has any money to buy formula."

The child had been left with a neighbor while the mother waited at the clinic for treatment. He'd only had water, no milk, for the past few days, and he was dying. They had taken him to the camp clinic and the doctor tried to put an IV in, but his tiny veins were too small and he was too dehydrated. They were told to take him home to die with his father. That was when my friends began to pray, and within an hour I was back at the camp.

"But I am not a doctor or a nurse," I insisted.

"No, you are Mama Delilah," Beyan said, as if that gave me magical healing powers. I almost chuckled thinking of my biological daughter back at home in the US, chronically ill with an autoimmune disorder and constantly in the hospital. How I wished I had the gift of healing.

My exhaustion fled, and I was suddenly energized. I took the tiny, lifeless infant into my arms. He took raspy, faint breaths that seemed to require all of his body's energy. I prayed. Debbie prayed. We all prayed. His big glassy eyes rolled back in his head then fluttered closed.

Suddenly I remembered a woman I had cared for earlier in the day, a young mother who was at the clinic. Her baby girl suffered from malaria and was too weak to nurse. As a result, the mother's breast had become inflamed with mastitis. I spent a bit of time with her, showing her how to express the milk by hand to relieve the pressure, how to put warm rags on her engorged breasts to reduce the swelling. She was only a few yards away from where we were standing. I told Debbie my plan, and, clutching the baby, we ran to her.

"We need to borrow your breast milk," I explained when we located her. She looked shocked but agreed.

We went through our bag of supplies and found rubber gloves, a syringe, and a water bottle. I took the cap off the bottled water while Debbie removed the needle from the syringe. I then asked the mother to express a tiny bit of milk into the bottle cap. She did.

We hesitated a moment, knowing that the mother should have been tested for HIV before we used her milk, but we had no time to spare and no other options available. Debbie drew the milk up into the needle-less syringe and placed it carefully into the dying baby's mouth, slowly dripping the milk into his throat. We prayed out loud the entire time. We were afraid he would aspirate on the liquid, so we didn't force it, just gently offered it drop by drop. Again the young nursing mama filled the little bottle cap. Again Debbie administered the drip, drip, drip...

The baby's raspy breathing was a rattle that shook his featherlight body and reminded me of my mom as she lay in her bed dying from brain cancer. His limbs were limp, his tongue was extended, and his lips were dark blue, almost black. The heaviness of his death rattle weighed more than that of his tiny spirit, it seemed.

A third capful and more prayers were offered—prayers in English and in Twi, in Ashanti and in the Liberian tribal tongues. Prayers for healing and prayers for life.

Suddenly, his head began to move. He flickered his eyes and briefly opened them. We prayed louder, and I pressed my ear to his tiny chest and listened for a heartbeat.

Fidel and Beyan had found Clarence, the father of the dying child, and brought him to us. He joined us in prayer and watched as the son he had said goodbye to an hour earlier began to move. His eyes, which had been rolled back, came forward and started to look around. The baby started breathing easier, and after what seemed like an eternity, he cried. We cried. We all cried and praised the Lord and cried some more!

One of the guards ran and got Tambor, the doctor who had tried to treat the child then sent him home to die with his family. Tambor was amazed and kept saying, "By

God's grace he lives! This cannot be the same baby I saw earlier! By God's grace he lives!"

Tambor led us to the mother, Bendu, who was almost as thin as her infant son. She was feverish and sweating, her beautiful face racked with pain. She was lying nearly naked on a filthy, unmade bed on the floor of the deplorable clinic, wrapped in a length of dirty batik and wearing a soiled shirt. Her stomach was swollen and hard and hot to the touch.

West Africa has a pay-as-you-go medical system. As war refugees, Bendu and her family had the privilege of being seen at the clinic in the refugee camp, and the doctors and nurses did the best that they could with such limited resources, but she could not be treated in the Ghanaian hospitals unless she could pay for the services. So she was at the clinic, dying of a mass that had become infected after she gave birth a few months before.

She was too weak to stand but cried tears of joy when she saw her son moving and breathing, his eyes bright once again.

"Take him," she begged. "Take him with you."

This wasn't the first time a mother had begged me to take her child, but usually it was in the hopes that if I took their child, I would care for them and send them money in exchange. But Bendu's expression and pleading were something entirely different. She knew she could not care for her baby, and she somehow knew I would not let the tiny infant die.

Tambor found someone to sell us formula and a baby bottle. I took the infant to a bench to continue feeding him and sat down to rest.

What had just happened?

A moment later, the mother who had donated the breast milk sat down beside me. Her baby had gotten medicine for her malaria and was now nursing once again.

We sat there in silence together, she with her daughter and me with the emaciated boy with the bright eyes. She was young and thin, and her skin was ebony. I was in my late forties, and my ample flesh was ivory. Two mamas who spoke entirely different languages, but who shared the universal language of motherhood.

As I sat there in the moonlight, I marveled.

How God had taken a girl from the farms of Oregon, an uneducated woman whose great grandfather on her mama's side had in all probability been a member of the Ku Klux Klan and whose father had disowned her for marrying a black man in 1982, and made her "Mama Delilah" to an entire village of African refugees?

I didn't grasp it then. I still don't.

I sat on that bench and wondered, *why me?* Maybe in that moment, I did not grasp it, but what I did grasp and have always known is that I could try to change the world for good, even if by one heart at a time.

∾

I love to pray. About everything. I pray for parking spots at the mall during the holidays, for planes to be held when I'm running late, for all the eggs to hatch when my chickens are sitting on a clutch, and I pray for my children to be healed of chronic and terminal illnesses.

When I begged God to spare my son Sammy's young life, to heal him, His answer was no. My anger and rage burned. My sorrow nearly swallowed me alive. And then I prayed for God to lift my pain enough for me to be able to breathe. In time, I realized that Sammy hurt. Every single day of his life, the sickle cell anemia caused him immense pain. I had to release my rage and accept God's will for my son, though I vehemently disagreed.

One of my favorite writers, C. S. Lewis, was quoted as saying, "I pray because I can't help myself. I pray because I'm helpless. I pray because the need flows out of me all the time—waking and sleeping. Prayer doesn't change God—it changes me."

I used to pray to change God's mind, or rather, to convince the Lord to see things my way. Sometimes I still do, but not nearly as often as before. Now I usually pray to know God's will in my life. I say "usually," because let's be honest, I still think God should see things my way sometimes... I'm only human.

I pray when I'm happy; I try to notice details in the natural world and in the things man has created and say a simple thank-you when I take note of God's handiwork. A sky painted orange and gold as the sun sets, the same sky blackened with powerful storm clouds that give rain to nurture my gardens... a pink rose, delicate with dew drops, the ridiculous noises my geese or miniature donkeys make... the smile in my daughter's eyes when I rub her back or massage her shoulders, the rhythmic breathing of my stubborn son Zack, who all but shut me out during the day, then looked like my last-born baby, peaceful and sweet, when I would check in on him before going to bed at night. For all these things I try to thank my God, and each day I look for new gifts and miracles to be grateful for. I have taken tens of thousands of photographs of the flowers, fruits, animals, and settings of my farm, recording the minuscule miracles that delight my eyes. Each picture, a praise to God for His creative powers.

For some, prayer is a tradition or a ritual that brings them peace and serenity, but for me it is life's breath. Some use prayer or rosary beads, memorized words or chants or a set time during the day to help establish a prayer routine. Me, not so much...

My deepest prayers are usually prayed when I'm outside enjoying the beauty of nature. It is in the quiet of the forest or sitting next to a stream that my mind is clear and I can meditate on God's holiness and His word. To try to grasp that the One who created the heavens and earth desires to connect and communicate with me is both humbling and empowering. When the world shoots me down, when honors and awards I have worked hard for go to others, when lovers leave, friends disappoint, my own body betrays and pain is searing, the fact that the Almighty values me enough to invite me into his presence to converse and connect is proof that I am valuable, precious, and loved.

The best time for me to pray? Anytime. Paul said, "Rejoice always. Pray continually." (1 Thess. 5:16-17) I wake up praying, asking God to give me wisdom as I start my day. I ask Him for favor and protection over all I say and do. Before I open my eyes, I try to praise Him in my heart and thank Him for the many challenges I will face throughout the day. (And to give me strength not to throttle those who annoy me!) I have a tendency to think that just because my motives are good, I have a green light to plunge ahead on a given course or project, and in doing so I have done more harm than good on more than one occasion. I need to pray for God to take the lead and let me know when and how far to go, and to give me the patience and wisdom to wait.

I pray during the day, less formally than you would guess. When I'm on horseback, I can spend hours in prayer. Me, my horse Shadow, and God wandering through the forests or racing down the beach. If someone were listening, they would think I am mad the way I talk out loud to the Lord! I shout praises when I see something spectacular, like a bald eagle circling my farm. I know it's looking for one of my chickens to steal, but I feel privileged to be able to see such a magnificent creature up close! I pray when my little kids are five minutes late getting home from school, and I pray when the older ones get behind the wheel of a car. I whisper prayers of protection when my son Isaiah and stepdaughter Rene are working as police officers, and prayers of gratitude when they go home after a twelve- or fifteen-hour shift.

I fall asleep most nights praying. I don't count sheep (at the present time I have three, however)—I count my blessings. I replay encounters that occurred during the day that I know were orchestrated by God.

Prayer elevates me from bouts of depression, grounds me during bouts of hysteria. Prayer deepens my faith and allows me clarity when my world is muddled and confused. Prayer lifts me from the mundane into the sublime at times. When I recognize that there is nothing I can do to affect or alter the course of others who are hell-bent on destruction, prayer gives me serenity and peace.

ONE HEART AT A TIME

Even if you have not reached a place where you can say "Heavenly Father" with true conviction that some power greater than yourself is listening, try praying anyway. If you have no faith, ask God to give it to you. If you don't believe, ask Him to reveal Himself to you. You can't get in trouble with God the way I used to think. When I heard people talking about prayer, I thought of it in the abstract, like an incantation or holy rite that had to be performed to perfection. I had seen paintings and artifacts that were religious in nature—the Virgin Mary kneeling in prayer with a halo of light above her head, saints in long robes with pious faces, eyes closed in prayer. Faith, before I really had any, was shrouded in symbols and a language I could not understand. And prayer was even more of a secret language, like the absurd passwords and handshakes of a secret society.

Matthew 18:2–5 says, "He called a little child to him, and placed the child among them. And he said: 'Truly I tell you, unless you change and become like little children, you will never enter the kingdom of heaven. Therefore, whoever takes the lowly position of this child is the greatest in the kingdom of heaven. And whoever welcomes one such child in my name welcomes me.'"

God wants us to forget the dogma, the religious hoops people have been jumping through for decades, and come with the open heart of a child. If you don't have the ability to conjure up enough faith to open your heart to God, then simply pray that He will reveal Himself in a very real way, with signs that won't make sense to anyone else but you.

My friend Lillian whispered such a prayer when her life was falling apart and she needed proof that a higher power could be called upon. She asked God to show her that He was real. A day later she came home to find her landlord had done some simple repairs to her small apartment kitchen and replaced some parts that were broken on her stove. When she walked in, she noticed a subtle change in the room and started crying. It wasn't the repairs on the stove. She noticed the plain metal knobs on the cupboards were also gone, replaced with antique ceramic knobs, festooned with pink-painted roses—the same knobs she had admired in her grandma's kitchen cupboards years before. The grandma who had taken Lillian in as a child when her alcoholic father came home in a drunken rage and beat her and her mother. The same grandma who taught her to cook and sew, and who shared her deep faith in Christ over hot tea and cakes. As Lillian grew older, she rejected her grandmother's faith and sought to find peace and self-worth in academics. She was working on her doctorate and writing her thesis when she took my challenge and asked God to show her He had heard her prayers.

Antique rose-painted knobs probably over a hundred years old warming up her tiny kitchen. A simple change, nothing earthshaking like a burning bush or a parted sea. She hadn't asked the landlord to change them, nor had he asked her if she was dissatisfied with the old ones. God answered her in a way that she instantly recognized, a sign that would have meant absolutely nothing to anyone else, but it transported Lillian's highly educated mind back to a simpler time sipping tea with her grandma.

Before my son Sammy passed away, he put his hands in the shape of a heart and pointed to me, then to my husband Paul. After the doctors worked frantically to save Sammy's

ONE HEART AT A TIME

life but could not stop his heart from failing, he left his sick, pain-filled body and walked into the arms of God.

When the doctors let us into the operating room to say goodbye, his hands were on his belly, still in the shape of a heart. Now when I am struggling or missing him, I whisper a prayer to let Sammy know he is loved. Sometimes, even within the hour, I am led to something heart-shaped in nature, a seashell on the beach or a sandstone on the path. Signs from God that my son's spirit lives on. I've taken hundreds of photos of these heart-shaped love letters from God. Heart-shaped clouds, heart-shaped stones on the beach—one day I might publish all of the little hidden signs that I've noticed from above.

Prayer is one of the most precious and yet powerful gifts bestowed to all of us on this planet. Anyone can do it, anytime, anywhere, anyhow. It's our direct line to heaven, a cordless communication with God Almighty, and He always answers the call! Perhaps not in the way we expect or think, but He hears us—every time, all the time. So why not take advantage of it more often? God has directed us to *pray without ceasing*, and I think that means He wants us to get chatty and include Him in our daily activities.

You should note, however, there is a counterpart to the praying life, and it's called the obedient response. Sometimes I go for months without any specific directive, urge, or feeling from God. And sometimes the urge is so strong, I can't deny what I should do. Take the trip back to an African refugee camp after dark and pray over a tiny baby on the brink of death. *Why?* Because someone that night needed to witness a miracle. Because that baby boy has a bigger purpose than I know. Because the story would plant a seed of faith in another villager who heard it. Because... there could be a hundred trickle-effect reasons why our prayers were answered that night. All I know for a fact is God told me to go back, and that's the only justification I need. What else I know is this: when you start talking to God, be ready when He starts talking back.

CHAPTER 5:
A HEART THAT SERVES

The day I was inspired to start Point Hope, in the early 1990s, is burned into my memory like the record-high temperature that day seared into my skin.

It was a hot, sticky July day, the kind that causes your hair to mat and stick to your neck and forehead. It was easily ninety-eight degrees. I was in the Inner Harbor area of Baltimore, walking back to the hotel room my friend Donna had rented for a real estate conference she was attending. She invited my young son Sonny and I to come along. My husband at the time, Doug, had elected to stay home. The temperature that day was an anomaly. There was a record heat wave on the East Coast. People actually fried eggs on the hoods of their cars or the sidewalks just to watch it happen.

As Sonny and I headed back to our room after a trip to the aquarium, watching tourists ride paddle boats on the harbor, I noticed a young woman. She was around my age, thirty-two at the time, and sitting on the curb in the direct sun, her bleached hair pulled back in a neat pony-tail. She was begging for money. She didn't look stoned or drunk, nor did she appear to be mentally ill. She just looked hot and hungry.

I wasn't used to homeless people. I hadn't had a lot of experience with them. In the tiny town in Oregon where I grew up, we didn't have homeless people—if somebody was homeless, they went and stayed with their moth-er, brother, sister, or friend. There were a few folks who might stay at the campsite in their trailers when they were down on their luck, but we did not have what is known as a homelessness problem. We had a few town bums and drunks that everyone knew and watched out for, but no one was living on the streets.

After I left Reedsport, I lived in middle-class neigh-borhoods in apartments or fixer-upper houses I could af-ford. I always lived outside cities in quiet neighborhoods with small dogs in fenced yards or in apartment buildings with lots of kids and noise and the smells of barbecue waft-ing up from the neighbors' small decks on a hot summer day. When I lived in Eugene and then Seattle, I was aware that some people were homeless. I would see them, mostly older men who were clearly alcoholics or disabled veterans, who would beg for money on the street corners. I would give them whatever loose change I had, smile, wish them well, and walk on without giving them another thought. Like many, I assumed they were homeless by choice—that they had chosen drugs or alcohol or other addictions over having a place to live. But this woman didn't fit any of those descriptions. I needed to know more.

I engaged my gift of gab and I sat down next to her. I started asking her questions. It's what I do—not just on the air, but always. People fascinate me, and the more complex their situations seem, the more intrigued I become. Here sat an attractive, articulate woman, begging for money. As her story unfolded, so did my heart.

This particular woman, whose name, I learned, was Cheryl, piqued my interest on this particularly hot summer day. After some time sweating with her in the hot sun, I learned she was a single mom who had fled an abusive marriage and ended up homeless as a result. I invited her and her two kids to join us for dinner. That afternoon, that conversation, changed me and set the course for the rest of my life.

When I invited her to dinner, I forgot it wasn't my hotel room, my credit card, or my event (I tend to do this). It was Donna's weekend and I probably should have consulted with her first... Instead I brought a homeless woman and her dirty-faced children back for dinner, and we ordered pizza and salads.

I knew from that point on I wanted to help the hopeless, and I started to talking to friends back home in Philadelphia, including Donna, about how we could share God's love with people like Cheryl. That was when I decided to start a nonprofit organization to help people, in tandem with my radio career.

After a record week of hundred-plus-degree temps, I went to the public library (which had the air-conditioning

I couldn't afford) and researched the coolest spot in America. The result: Point Hope, Alaska. While the asphalt was melting in Philly, it was a cool fifty-two degrees in Point Hope that day.

I had a burst of inspiration. I sketched out a script, then called my program director, Leigh Jacobs, to get permission to do a mock-remote broadcast. That evening, using sound effects and a good producer, I "flew" to Point Hope, Alaska, while on the air!

On this mock trip, I described for listeners the wind-swept tundra, the herds of wild caribou and flocks of terns that I could see beneath the wings of the Cessna seaplane I was pretending to be flying in. The sound of sea birds screeching and sea lions barking were broadcast "live," as my producer had access to a great sound-effects library. I described the cool wind on my face when we landed and got out of the plane. The chunks of blue ice floating off the shoreline. The amazing breeze that called for a light windbreaker.

Sitting in that cramped radio studio in Bala Cynwyd, Pennsylvania, with three books about Alaska I had just checked out of the Radnor public library, I created a cool oasis for five hours on the air. Almost all of what I broadcast was made up on the spot, with the exception of a few facts woven in. It was fly-by-the-seat-of-your-pants radio, and it was so much fun! It wasn't just me having a great time. My phone lines lit up even more than usual. Even my friends Judy and Donna called the hotline demanding to know when I had flown to Alaska!

That was one of the most creative and energizing shows I've ever done. With it, I not only elevated my BS skills to a new level, I landed the name for the nonprofit organization I was going to create to help the homeless. *Point Hope.*

The concept of Point Hope was simple: meet homeless people in their environment and talk to them. We didn't set out to evangelize or hand out religious tracts. We took to the streets of downtown Philadelphia in search of pockets of homeless people to whom we'd serve a humble meal of tuna fish sandwiches (after all, Jesus fed the masses with fishes and loaves) and ice-cold lemonade.

My garage, dining room, and living room soon turned into collection sites for shoes, shirts, coats, and blankets. In addition to handing out sandwiches and lemonade, we began handing out bags full of clothes, shampoo, soaps, and, in the harsh winter months, blankets, coats, and boots.

After my experience with Cheryl, I wanted to meet these vagabonds. I wanted to learn what led them to the streets, and why they had no family to take them in. Why they didn't have Section 8 housing or a best friend who could take them in, especially if they had young children. I wanted to share a sandwich, but also let each person know they had great value. That regardless of the circumstances that led them to sleeping in a cardboard box beneath a freeway, they had worth and that God loved them.

Donna, my roomie/bestie/producer Janey, and I and a handful of others met every Wednesday morning in my kitchen and made hundreds of sandwiches. We started our day at the art museum and walked the exact same route each week. After the second or third trip, we noticed a handful of the folks from the previous week would be expecting us. By the end of September, we had dozens of friends waiting for us. They laughed, joked, and teased us each week. We knew them by name and over time got to know their stories and personalities.

I would sort the piles of clothes in my living room during the week and think, "Clarence would love this topcoat," or "Angeline would look pretty in this pink sweater." I'd set aside the things I thought each person would enjoy, and soon they came to anticipate the individual gifts.

At first I tried to enlist the help of a few local churches and organizations, but because we were not an official 501(c)(3) and did not have tax-exempt status, many refused. Some who did want to join us had their own specific agendas and wanted to proselytize and evangelize. That was not a part of our goal or mission. I wanted to share the love of God, to pass on the blessings I had been given, and to share my faith in deeds.

To some of my non-Christian, free-spirited friends I invited to help (okay, begged and harangued), I seemed too religious. Because I'm a Christian and believed it was the love of Christ that called me to share my time and resources, many of my nonbelieving friends shied away. But because I'm not your typical evangelist and my language is often peppered with words that any churchgoing grandma would find offensive (along with my tattoos), most church leadership also passed on the opportunity to join us. I wasn't religious enough for them.

I'll admit, I had a pretty fairy-tale notion about those who were homeless back then. I thought if someone respected them, gave them a hand up as opposed to a handout, they would be able to plug back into society and change their situation. After two years and thousands of tuna fish sandwiches, I realized the problem of homelessness was far beyond my understanding, and I certainly had no tools or power to fix it. But I did meet some amazing, colorful people who had talent, insights, survival skills, and, mostly, laughter.

I met old folks with faces more lined than a map of Philly, and young men and women; prostitutes and heroin addicts; drunks and druggies; and children with hollow eyes and sunken cheeks. Many of the homeless were mentally ill, and as we became friends, I got to know each person, their fears, and their passions, and in extending myself and my gifts to them, I, and my friends, even if only temporarily, made a difference in their lives.

I have to brag on my friend Donna a little bit. We call her our fairy god-Donna. A small-framed woman in her forties when we met, she had never married nor had children of her own, so she spent a considerable amount of time and energy spoiling my son and other kids that she loved.

Donna is from a large family of Philadelphia Italians who lived, laughed, ate, and fought together. Her father and uncles lived in houses they'd built next to or across the street from their mother. One lived next door, the other a few yards behind Donna's house. When she was young, at least twenty cousins lived in the same neighborhood, and played stickball and roller-skated together.

Their family meals were epic, and, as she explained, Donna had inherited the Italian "need-to-feed-you gene." Donna plied us with crown roasts and crab feasts when all my budget could support was Top Ramen with scrambled eggs. Lucky for me and Sonny, we were adopted into this wonderful family when we moved to Philly in 1992.

Donna worked in title insurance and had a very successful business. A petite woman with huge doe-brown eyes, she has one of the best senses of humor of anyone I know. She had a perfectly decorated house at the Jersey Shore and drove a new, dark-green Mercedes. Every six weeks, she had her hair done by Mina, another feisty Italian, and she wore smart Italian leather shoes. Her hair was neat, her car was spotless, her house was clean and comfortable, and her life was tidy. That is, until she decided to reach out to the crazy lady on the radio (yours truly) to play a practical joke on a friend.

Donna was a listener who heard me talking over the air about the not-so-practical jokes I loved to pull on family and friends. We get insane when it comes to jokes. *Insane.* From hiding someone's car in another town to climbing on a girlfriend's roof and shouting down the chimney that God is watching them to filling a friend's thermos with overcooked pasta and telling them it was worms to delivering hillbillies on horses to a five-star art gallery during opening night of my first art gallery showing, my friends and I love to prank one another.

One night Donna called the request line wanting to get involved with our pranks. She had a pretty fun story to share about someone she knew showing up at the airport wearing nothing but a raincoat and high heels to meet a boyfriend who was part of the military brass—only to have security pull her aside and demand that she remove the coat!

A few days later I met Donna in person for the first time. We met in the parking lot so I could take possession of two live turkeys, which she had gotten as a gag gift for her birthday just days before. We arranged to deliver the birds on Thanksgiving Day to an unsuspecting friend of mine named Judy. The box was labeled "Vermont Teddy Bear." The Vermont Teddy Bear Company makes awesome teddy bears. They're handmade, adorable, customized teddy bears, and the company had advertised them on my show. As a gift bonus, they sent a handmade bear to my son. I used the big box, filled it with paper and straw, and gently tucked the gobblers inside. When my messenger arrived at Judy's town house, the top was closed and the box was handed off to a woman who was shocked to feel it move as she took possession of it...

The birds were safely released to a sanctuary, but that evening set the tone for many years of hilarity that followed. Over the past twenty-four years, Donna and I have pulled pranks on one another and pretty much everyone in our circle of friends. Judy retaliated for the birds by filling my tub, bathroom, and bedroom waist-deep with balloons while I was visiting family on the West Coast. Another time I returned home to find all my furniture gone; my living room and dining room had been emptied of furniture and in its place was a ton of beach sand and a boom box playing the Beach Boys tune "Surfin' USA." Instead of my thrift store couch, cobbled-together antiques, and self-upholstered love seat, I found a Delilah dummy made of a stuffed T-shirt and leggings with a blond wig lying next to a kiddie pool filled with water, and on the ceiling overhead there was a kite suspended in midair trailing a sign that read "Welcome to Gotcha-Back Beach"!

One of the craziest pranks to date came when I got fired from Philadelphia's WMGK in 1994 and had to move back to Boston to take a job there. Donna and my business manager at the time, Fred, arranged to have fifty-two bowling balls packed in my moving boxes. I didn't discover what they had done until I had lugged the fifth or sixth unusually heavy box up the two flights of stairs in the rambling old Victorian house I was moving into—in the middle of a Boston blizzard. One box was marked "attic," the next was marked "kitchen," and I couldn't figure out for the life of me why each box weighed a ton! There were bowling balls in an old ice chest, in boxes of spices and kitchen pots, in with my toiletries and my son's toys.

I stood there, in a blizzard, my newborn daughter wrapped in four layers of clothes and blankets, confused out of my mind as to why Doug had collected so many damned bowling balls! It wasn't until the umpteenth trip up the stairs that it dawned on me I'd been pranked again.

Oh, God, what a sense of humor You have. You must! Because when I think back to what my love for pranks has begun, I'm amazed at how even the silliest form of expression has spiraled into something so much bigger than me. Pranks that led to on-air fodder that led to a friendship with another prankster, fairy god-Donna, that led to a weekend in Maryland that led to Cheryl on the street in the sweltering sun that led me to Point Hope, Alaska—which gave a name to my nonprofit, Point Hope, and a whole new perspective on our homeless population. Point Hope has since taken off into orphan care, refugee care, and foster care, expanding its reach to help many folks in need domestically and abroad.

Sometimes God just lines it up for you. All those pranksters I speak of, most of them have been on the board for Point Hope, channeling their creativity in other ways that tremendously bless people. And while I still love a good prank story, I also love hearing how someone who was offered a hand up dug themselves out of despair, or how a volunteer, much like my younger self, is changed after being exposed to the orphan care crisis in a refugee camp.

If you have a heart for helping others, and you're a praying person, don't be surprised one day when God lines it up for you, too. When all of a sudden your heart is pierced with the truth about a situation that drives you to crave more information and to finally get involved. You'll feel it, much like I felt it that day sitting with Cheryl on that scorching-hot sidewalk in Maryland. You'll want to help. And when you do realize you're ready to serve others, God will make a way, if He's not already doing so in your life.

What you'll come to realize is when you serve others, when you volunteer even a little bit, your life will be blessed. No, it probably won't make you wealthy, but you'll be richly blessed with joy. For the Bible says...

> "He who is kind to the poor lends to the LORD, and He will reward him for what he has done." Proverbs 19:17

Delilah

> *"He who gives to the poor will lack nothing, but he who closes his eyes to them receives many curses." Proverbs 28:27*

> *"Jesus answered, 'If you want to be perfect, go, sell your possessions and give to the poor, and you will have treasure in heaven. Then come, follow me.'" Matthew 19:21*

Search the Internet for Bible verses about caring for the poor and the needy, and you'll find more than you bargained for. Read those passages, and it will become clear how this life should work.

God wants us to care for the most vulnerable in our society, and if that means you step up to help, *you will lack nothing*. Because He cares for you, too. And that, my friends, is no joke…

CHAPTER 6:
A HEART THAT IS FREE

My father was a study in contradictions; his entire life was one big contradiction, and within those contradictions were hidden both the secrets of his brilliance, humor, and talent, and the demons that sought to destroy him.

Dad was brilliant, one of the smartest men I've ever met. Even though he was a high-school dropout with learning disabilities, he later returned to community college and became an engineer at a nearby electrical Public Utility Department, where he spent the majority of his career. He had the ability to calculate dimensions, square feet, angles, and radius without measuring tools. He could look at a building and accurately estimate how many feet of lumber it would take to build it, how thick the footings would need to be poured, and what kind of electrical service would need to be installed. Outside work, his hobbies included designing and building houses and boats, small engine repair, and making silly but functional things like popcorn poppers and rock tumblers. He was an amazing craftsman and woodworker. But as brilliant as he was, he was incredibly insecure and could never figure out how his controlling behavior led those he loved and cared for to pull away from him instead of lean toward. He felt like a victim, resentment and anger being his foremost emotions.

Dad was funny—he could tell jokes and weave together ridiculous stories that would send everybody off in gales of laughter. His humor was usually politically incorrect, off-color, and on point. He knew how to draw you in, draw the punch line out, raise and lower his voice at just the right times, and could invoke crazy accents and inflections to get his audience fully hooked. He could be a good listener, a great advice giver, a mentor and a friend. He was charismatic and an absolute people magnet when he was in a good mood.

He danced, he sang, and he played the guitar in a country-western band. When Dad was happy, he had a song in his heart and a lilt to his step. Any time we asked him a simple question, he would answer with the lyrics from a song. He loved fifties rock and roll, swing, big band, and western music. He could sing along with Elvis, Waylon, Buddy Holly, or the Platters.

Dad could twist, jitterbug, do the Tennessee Bird Walk and the Watusi, and he never seemed to tire on the dance floor despite his decades-long habit of smoking unfiltered cigarettes. Or so we heard. I rarely saw his dancing skills firsthand, as he and Mom would head out at night with best friends Bob, Doris, Carl, and Ann. The six of them would find a bar with a live band, or the men would play (all three were guitarists) while the women sang and danced. They laughed and partied till the sun came up then drove home to find kids asleep in piles of blankets on the couch, a carton of ice cream gone and bowls of popcorn spilled on the floors.

We *loved* this Dad when he sang and danced, when he played the guitar, when he and his well-lubricated buddies went off to the garage and made metal art or performed open-heart surgery on my sister's broken dolly while the moms played nursey. He was animated, larger than life, our music-filled hero.

Then, like a light switch that was flipped, he would change. One day he would wake up singing and silly, and the next he would come home dark and brooding. We never knew what precipitated the change from dancing blue eyes and little ditties to the storm clouds of discontent. But when Dad changed, the entire house was smothered in darkness.

Mom would turn silent, watching with her worried green eyes for a sign as to how bad the storm would be and how long it would take to pass. She smoked more, snapped and pointed her fingers at us kids to make us sit down, be quiet, stop horsing around, be still. Her lips would purse to thin worried lines, her eyebrows knitting together above her straight nose. Her broad, strong face would turn to granite and be filled with fear of the damage that she knew could come with the dark clouds swirling about my father. The damage came in waves of deafening silence, sometimes outbursts of uncontrolled rage, usually directed toward Mom or Matt and me. When Dad would turn, he became icy cold and calculating. He would brood, plot, and stalk our mom. He would withhold affection, withhold finances.

When Dad was happy, everyone was happy. We talked about school, and often Dallen, our neighbor and my brother's best friend, would be at the table with us. On relaxed days, our dad would do something unexpected, like pinch the middle from his dinner roll (to form a pocket for butter and jam) and pitch it at someone at the other end of the table, creating screams of laughter.

We kids always had kitchen duty afterward. My dad would supervise with a full cup of coffee, a cigarette, and his feet up on the corner of the table. If it was a roll-pitching night, we'd bravely tie his shoelaces together and then startle him awake. I think we actually got him once, but he'd play along pretending to trip dozens and dozens of times. After dishes, if the weather was nice, we'd head outside to play and sometimes go to the beach.

But when Dad was in one of his moods, we sat in awkward silence at the table, followed our routines, tried desperately to remember our manners, never complained, and asked to be excused as quickly as possible. Mom sat next to Dad so she could jump up from the table and get him fresh coffee or more potatoes when he indicated he wanted them.

Dishes on these days were never done to his satisfaction. On more than one occasion he pulled all the pots and pans out of the cupboard and demanded we wash them all over again. The floor wasn't clean enough, and the oven needed to be scrubbed. Even prearranged activities had to wait, driving us to events was a terrible inconvenience, and we lived with a pit in our stomachs wondering what the punishment would be, and to whom would it be meted out.

Punishment came in waves of deafening silence, or several whacks across our bums with his leather belt. The strangest things would cause a volcanic explosion when he was in the midst of his darkness... a misplaced screwdriver in his workshop, a woodpile not stacked to his satisfaction, a garbage can left without a liner, tomatoes missing from the salad, Mom arriving ten minutes late from a dentist appointment...

By the time I was in high school, the father I had grown up with seemed to be long gone. My sister, DeAnna, had a different relationship with him and has much different memories, but my father had all but disappeared for me. When I reached ninth grade, he and Mom had become strangers living beneath the same roof pretending to be married. Mom chose me as her confidante and shared her frustrations, fears, desperation, and secrets. She wanted to leave; she cried for hours about fears and her misery, but she had neither the courage nor the life skills to go. I felt flattered to be her confidante and looked at my father through different eyes—her eyes. In retrospect, it wasn't fair to me. I took on her attitude of frustration and contempt. I think it was opposite for DeAnna. She had always been a daddy's girl. Though he did not confide in her, like my mom in me, she was more empathetic to his pain and drew closer to him trying to protect what she only knew intuitively was his fragile soul.

Dad knew Mom was angry, desperate, and unhappy, which caused his depression to grow and his moods to worsen. Looking back, it really was quite tragic that two people who loved one another so fiercely could not communicate or express their needs to one another, so they lived in complete misery.

Dad had dozens of inventions, hundreds of plans, and more schemes than a leopard has spots. Had he followed through on any of them, he probably would have been wealthy, even famous. But his brilliance and talents were squelched by his doubts and fears. For some people alcohol destroys their gifts; for Dad it seemed to fuel his creativity. When sober, his boldness and his creativity gave way to headaches and smokes. He was never a mean or obnoxious drunk, nor do I remember his good friends ever being mean or out of control. Thankfully, all I remember are the songs they sang late into the night as the stars twinkled overhead.

When I was sixteen, I found out my father had been married before our mom. A girlfriend had become pregnant when she was sixteen and he was nineteen. They had a daughter, Maddalyn, whom he apparently adored. Soon after her birth, his young wife's old boyfriend reentered the scene. The marriage was soon over. Turned out, however, she was once again pregnant. Kenneth was born twelve months after Maddalyn, to divorced parents. My father never believed Ken was his (this was long before DNA tests), and some time after his wife remarried and he had married my mother, he relinquished his parental rights. Although my half siblings lived in the same community I grew up in, we never knew they existed until we were emergent adults.

The kids were adopted by their stepfather and carried his name, not ours. Maddy and Ken Watson were my father's dark secret, something that he hid from the world. Whether it was the unplanned pregnancy, the young marriage, or the divorce that was the source of his great shame, I don't know. We never discussed it as long as he lived. I was told of his first family in secret by my mother's parents when Dad and I were having one of our epic rows. But I do believe it was this secret and the overwhelming pain of being disconnected from the children he loved that was at the root of his depression and manic behaviors.

On the Thursday before Memorial Day 1985, our family was dealt a devastating blow when my brother, Matt, and his wife, Anne, disappeared in the small plane he was piloting. It wasn't until five years later that the wreckage was finally found. We were then able to have a memorial service for them and some closure to our living hell. My half brother, Ken, whom I'd met not long before losing Matt, contacted me and asked if he could attend the service. I didn't know how to respond. Dad had disowned me years earlier because he felt I'd dishonored our family by marrying a black man. It wasn't my place to invite Ken or to tell him he couldn't attend; I wasn't even sure what would happen when I showed up.

A few weeks later, I attended the graveside service. As I stood outside my car, Ken approached me and gave me a hug. He looked sheepish and nervous; he'd never even met Matthew, even though they had attended the same small community college at the same time. As we stood talking, he looked at my father, walking toward the enclosure. "Is that him?" Ken asked. It was then I realized this young man, in his thirties, at his half brother's funeral, had never met his father.

Awkwardly I approached my father, leading Ken by the hand. I hadn't seen Dad in a few years and wasn't sure how he would react. "Ken, meet your father. Dad, meet your son Ken," I said, then turned and left the two of them standing together. Ken was the spitting image of our father, and if Dad had ever questioned whether he was the actual father or not, the answer was obvious when he looked at his son's face and saw his younger reflection.

A few minutes later, the oldest of my father's six children, Maddy, arrived with her two boys. My dad must have thought he entered hell that day. Our mother had finally—by having an affair with an old family friend—gathered the courage to leave him just months earlier. My dad was stricken by his collapsed marriage, the grief of losing Matt, and the shock of meeting his adult children and grandchildren, but also from the sadness of shutting a door to me and being too stubborn to realize it could be easily opened again.

Dad was a stubborn, prideful man. Once he made a declaration, he felt he had no option but to stick with it. When he disowned me, even though I know from what he told others he regretted it, he was too prideful to retract it. Luckily, he did open his heart to Ken and Maddy in the last few years of his life. He not only formed a relationship with the two children he had lost touch with, but he was able to spend a great deal of time with his grandchildren before he passed. I pray that gave him comfort and peace and he was able to finally let go of the terrible secret that poisoned his heart for far too long.

Dad was only fifty-seven when he died. He weighed less than one hundred pounds, I am told—lung disease had robbed him of his music, his laughter, his ability to walk more than a few feet without gasping for oxygen. Whether it was the cigarettes or the chemicals in the mills he worked in as a young man that destroyed his lungs, or faulty genetics (as my daughter and I both have weak lungs), I don't know. Honestly, I think his early demise had more to do with the pain of keeping secrets and the poison that comes from bitter regrets. Dad loved fiercely but was filled with regrets. He never learned to swallow his pride and say, "I'm sorry, I was wrong." He was a genius who was a fool, a builder who tore down what he loved the most, a talented musician who couldn't find the words to the songs in his heart.

Joe Cocker recorded a wonderful song in the eighties called "Letting Go." I've played it hundreds of times on my radio show for people who are trying to move forward, trying to let go of a toxic person, a marriage, or even a memory, and free their hearts to move forward. The chorus strikes a chord in my heart:

> *Letting go,*
> *Letting go,*
> *The hardest part is knowing*
> *That I'll miss you so.*
> *I'd like to wish you well,*
> *Hey but it hurts you know,*
> *Sometimes doing what is right*
> *Means letting go...*

Sometimes doing what is right means letting go— letting go of the memories that hold our hearts captive, or letting go of relationships that are toxic to gain back our serenity.

Many years ago—in fact, a few years before that song was released—I went for a hot-air balloon ride as part of a radio promotion. My son Isaiah was only a toddler and probably can't remember being hoisted with me into the big woven basket. As the brightly colored balloon filled with hot air, the balloonist who held our lives in his hands explained the importance of the weighted sandbags that held the basket in place until the balloon was inflated enough to carry us skyward. When he said it was time to soar, the ropes were untied and we sailed heavenward. The seasoned balloonist explained that a few weeks prior to our outing, he had witnessed another balloonist trying to ascend, who neglected to untie all of the weighted sandbags from his craft. One rope held on, and the balloon was dragged down, with the balloonist and his passengers clinging to the tipping basket as it bounced awkwardly against the ground until at last the balloon was deflated and the basket came to rest upright. Luckily, no one was hurt, but it could have been a deadly disaster.

Sometimes memories or dysfunctional people who have a hold on our heart are like the sandbag that pulled the balloon precariously downward and nearly caused it to crash. And yet, even knowing our lives may depend upon it, letting go can be the hardest thing in the world to do. I have said in the past I never let go of anything that didn't have claw marks all over it...

If you walk through my farmhouse or my sister's home, you will notice knickknacks, framed prints, furniture from a bygone era. We aren't exactly collectors of antiques as much as we are collectors of things that remind us of our parents and grandparents. Because we lost our folks when we were still young adults, we tend to cling to anything that our family members once cherished. It doesn't matter if the thing was actually theirs or not—it only needs to resemble something that Mom would have had on a shelf in our family home or Grandma would have displayed in her kitchen, and we snatch it up from a garage sale or thrift store and carry it home to add to our growing piles of mothball-scented memories.

It doesn't stop with furniture and artwork on display in our living rooms; it spreads like English ivy to our kitchen cupboards, with embroidered linens, cast-iron skillets, milk-glass salt and pepper shakers, to our closets chock-full of antique hats, cat-eye glasses, rhinestone costume jewelry, vintage jackets and skirts that are over fifty years old. Even our gardens are living museums, with tea roses transplanted from Grandma's garden and fig trees and four-leaf clovers from Mom's backyard. Neither my sister nor I could ever live in a contemporary house with bare walls or minimalistic style; we could not release all of the memorabilia and relics we have hoarded like squirrels' nuts over the years.

Even harder for me is letting go of people I love but who are hurtful and destructive. I have heard at various twelve-step meetings I've attended that being in a relationship with an active addict is like being in a cage with a lion. As beautiful as the great cat is, you enter the cage knowing that at any moment, that beautiful creature can rip your head off your shoulders in an instant. Being in a relationship with someone who is an active addict—whether their addiction is to alcohol and drugs or behaviors like pornography or gambling—is putting yourself at risk of being ripped apart. Because someone who is an active addict can't really have a relationship with you; they can only use you to further their addiction.

And like the antique roosters that line my kitchen shelves, I seem to collect addicts and alcoholics aplenty. Husbands one and two, a few boyfriends, a drummer in a rock band, girlfriends from every town I've ever lived in, neighbors and nannies, and sadly a few of my grown children...

I was in my late twenties before I found my way to a room filled with other adults who loved people who loved alcohol. What a life-changing experience that was! Sitting with my peers, hearing my story told over and over, in different voices from different perspectives, but always the same outcome. Loving someone who loves booze more than they love themselves or others is hell. Loving someone who loves meth or crack or heroin more than they love themselves, more than they love life, more than they love the feel of their mama's hands on their feverish forehead, more than they love the sound of their baby's laughter, is worse than hell. Knowing the only way to survive is to walk away and pray they find their way back to sanity before they find their way to the grave is the hardest thing in the world to do. Especially when the one you must walk away from is one that you felt flutter to life in your belly, or one whose hand you held before the judge signed the adoption papers, whom you held at night when the storm raged outside, making sure they felt safe and secure in your loving embrace. To let go and let God watch over them as the storm of addiction batters them to and fro is to trust in a future that is not promised. But to try to fix, heal, control, or direct is as pointless as trying to yell at the wind to stop blowing or the waves to stop crashing.

There is a beautiful woman with curly, flaming-red hair and a lopsided smile I became friends with when my last-born biological son was a few weeks old. Her teenage son and mine were friends; she and her small family lived with her mother-in-law, a few houses down the street from ours. When my twelve-year-old son mentioned that Delilah on the radio was his mom, Tina (not her real name) didn't believe him. My son is black, and Tina knew from the publicity I had done that Delilah on the radio was a tall blonde. She argued with my son and said, "Delilah can't be your mom—she's white."

Laughing, my son said, "Yes, yes, she is my mom," and dragged Tina down to my house to meet me.

It was love at first sight; our friendship was instant and filled with laughter. As the months and years went by, our sister-like bond grew—our kids played together, we both went through difficult divorces. Tina found herself without a place to live. I had purchased a little house next to mine for my in-laws to move into when they retired, and since that was a while off, I made it available to Tina and her sons. The closer our friendship grew, the more I was troubled by my friend's bouts of drinking wine. Many nights she'd call me when I'd get off the air, her speech slurred and her laughter raucous. After a few years of living in my little house next to me, her older boy, who was developing his own addictions, had kicked in bedroom doors, broken the walls in several places, and smoked in my house. I was angry and frustrated. Tina left the house without holding him accountable and without apologies, and although our friendship was strained, we made it through that.

Fast-forward eight years to several more attempts at rescuing Tina and her sons from bad decisions, and many, many fights over the empty bottles of wine that piled up, the bills that went unpaid, and the chaos that followed her everywhere. In addition to red wine, her attraction to dysfunctional partners was insanely destructive. At one point, one of her partners refused to let my kids come and visit Tina's kids because they left footprints on the floors and fingerprints on her granite countertops.

We had been friends for years, gone on vacations together, and talked at least once a day, and she allowed her controlling lover to dictate the parameters of our relationship.

My frustration came to a head one day when she called to say she thought she had been poisoned, that two entire days were missing in her memory. I rushed to her house and drove her to the hospital. It was a Sunday afternoon. My red-haired friend seemed very lucid and coherent but couldn't remember anything from Friday afternoon on. At the hospital the police were called to begin an investigation into who had poisoned her. While we were waiting for the police to begin their questions, the doctor on duty came in the exam room and asked to speak with me privately. He pulled me out to the hall to tell me my friend's blood alcohol level was more than three times the legal limit. The doctor, obviously angry and annoyed, said she had not been poisoned—she had blacked out and lost memory from her drunkenness. And yet she showed no signs of obvious intoxication, no slurring, no stumbling, nothing to indicate she was out-of-her-mind drunk.

The trip home was a nightmare, and I hate to confess how badly I lost my temper and how inappropriately I behaved. I wanted to beat Tina and leave her stranded on the side of the road.

A few more years, a few more heartbreaks, and I realized the only thing I could do was let go. Not that I had any choice—she quit answering my calls and avoided me like the plague when she moved in with yet another crazy lover. I had to realize she wanted her booze and her freaky lovers more than she wanted a real relationship, more than she wanted to save her own life. Letting go isn't easy; I miss her every day and wonder why alcoholism can overwhelm and control such a funny, smart, incredible person to such a destructive degree, but it does.

Addiction is a cunning and baffling demon. It lies, it steals. It kills. It is no respecter of persons. It is not picky or prejudiced; it kills the brilliant and the slow-minded, the religious and the atheist, rich and poor, young and old.

I heard a famous female writer who had gotten sober say, "People said I abused alcohol. I never abused alcohol. I abused my family, my friends, myself, but never my alcohol... alcohol was all I cared about."

It's hard when you love someone completely, a spouse or a child, a parent or a best friend, to watch them destroy their body and their mind with drugs, alcohol, gambling, eating disorders, promiscuity, or sex addictions. Harder yet is letting go and letting God rescue or heal them. For some of us, we will let our wallets be stolen as well as our peace of mind, our houses assaulted as well as our bodies or our hearts before we finally admit we are powerless to stop the addict.

If I probed into your life over the phone, as is my job at night, chances are you would reveal to me, intentionally or not, something you need to let go of. If it's not something presently in your life, it was there in the past, or you'll have it in the future, I have no doubt. Life happens to all of us—wounds, hurt, and grievances… to live fully means we must let go.

For my dad, it was letting go of his secret life, the half siblings he hid from us. I believe that's the pain he wanted to sip away in the evenings and that kept him in a fog of depression. I heard a saying once—"You're only as sick as your secrets"—and how true it was for him. If he had let go of that secret, meaning brought his hidden family together with his current one, things might have been different, probably better, maybe worse. But at least the grip of that secret wouldn't have held him hostage for so long.

For me, it's letting go of the need to fix my friend Tina, as well as dozens of other people I love. From past husbands and lovers to adult children and friends, I have to let go of the need to rescue and trust that God will walk with them down the path that I cannot.

For others, it's letting go of anger and resentment, and offering forgiveness. My father couldn't admit he was wrong about turning his back to me, was too prideful to say he was sorry, too prideful to realize I would've embraced him in a heartbeat. And I believe it was ultimately the weight of the burdens he carried that crushed such a strong man far too young.

What are you holding on to that's making your soul sick with anger, depression, sadness, anxiety? You'll recognize it as the thing that's always there in the back of your mind, barring you from living a free and happy existence. If only that person were better, or if that issue was resolved, or if that memory didn't keep sneaking in... the enormous weight would be lifted. Maybe it's time to "let go and let God." Offer up prayers about that thing that weighs so heavily on you, and ask God to take it from here.

In the end, I'm not in your shoes and I can't make a judgment for you, but I've talked with enough people over the past forty years, perfect strangers, who've all had something in common—they have some form of sandbag they need to cut loose before they can soar. Ask God how to proceed in letting something go, offload the weight, and let him carry it going forward.

> *"Come to Me, all who are weary and heavy-laden, and I will give you rest."*
> *Matthew 11:28*

CHAPTER 7:
AN EMPOWERED HEART

I've always been my parents' daughter, unable to spend a hundred dollars on a blouse that could be sewn at home for five dollars, unwilling to buy furniture from a showroom when I can find a great couch at Goodwill for fifty dollars. Mom could take a well-worn dress from the thrift store or a garage sale, a scrap of fabric from the local dime store, add rickrack or lace and salvaged buttons from a vintage frock, and create a gorgeous dress for a prom or a wedding. Like Cinderella and the mice sewing ribbons onto a dress in the attic, Mom was able to create absolute beauty out of scraps. She sewed curtains, pillows, and bedspreads; she once decorated an entire room using a set of floral sheets from JCPenney. She and Dad never once owned a new car, never stayed in a four-star hotel, never shopped at Nordstrom or Macy's. They lived a simple life and enjoyed simple pleasures.

Mom would hear the neighbors had bagged a deer during hunting season, and she'd show up at their door with a huge metal tub and ask for the bones when the buck was butchered. She'd bring the bones home, put them in a pot of water on the stove and boil them for hours, adding salt, pepper, and garlic for taste, and then can the broth in quart jars. During the wet winter months she'd open a jar of soup stock and add a bag of noodles and some veggies, and we would have delicious, hot soup for dinner. She let nothing go to waste.

Dad was equally resourceful. He thought it was foolish to pay the $2.50 a week to have Hahn's Garbage Service pick up our trash. Instead he'd put the garbage can in the back of the truck and drive to the city dump. The dump had a section where people could leave household items and building materials that could be salvaged or reused. Washing machines that no longer spun the clothes, boats with holes in the bottom, bikes with flat tires and busted seats... this was the *real* reason for Dad's dump runs. Treasures waiting to be salvaged! Dad would throw a bike in the back of the truck, bring it home, and show me and my brother how to straighten the wheel and add new spokes, how to oil the chain and take out a link if it was too loose. How to take a seat apart so Mom could reupholster it, and how to hang it from the rafters with thin wire to spray paint it candy-apple red. We would add decals, streamers on the handle grips, and a piece of plastic in the spokes to make it sound like a motor! I had no clue

Dad was picking through others' trash, and there was no shame in our secondhand clothes or treasures.

My work ethic and commitment to excellence are all from my dad, as is my belief that going into debt limits your options in life. From him I learned that frugality and treading lightly on our environment has nothing to do with politics but more to do with the philosophy of "waste not, want not."

The only people more frugal than my parents were my grandparents.

My grandma McGowne washed her tinfoil from the Christmas turkey. She reused it. More than once. She washed out freezer bags that were filled with berries, hanging them with a plastic clothespin over her sink to dry and use again. And again. And again. Grandma had a drawer full of rubber bands, a tin can full of buttons, a freezer full of meat and berries, and a box full of worms to use as fishing bait. The dinner scraps went to Zip the golden lab; what he couldn't eat went to the worm box. She wasted nothing.

My sister, DeAnna, is the repurposing queen. Her entire house is decorated with repurposed furniture, salvaged frames, handmade curtains, mosaic stepping-stones, and beach glass. She took a welding class and fashioned her own veranda, bathroom fixtures, and yard art. Her talent knows no bounds, but unfortunately her small yard does have its limits and there's barely any room left for her found treasures.

My brother Tim rebuilds cars and trucks, remodels houses, and can pour cement like a pro. He can weld anything and build a boat or sand rail using leftover parts from a motor home, empty oil barrels, and a wrecked Volkswagen. His home is amazing—every inch was designed and built by him and his wife. Using salvaged materials and clever repurposing, it is a work of art.

To this day, I can't drive by a piece of furniture left by the side of the road, I have to stop and inspect it, decide if it is worth the effort to sand and stain and repurpose. Luckily, I have acres on which to store old washing machines that may one day be repaired, old bikes that need a can of candy apple–red paint and a new seat, and old baker's racks that can be turned into potting tables for my gardens. I repurpose used bed frames and turn them into benches to place in the forests and fields of my farm; I salvage lawn tools and turn them into garden art; old wine bottles become hummingbird feeders. When we butcher a cow, I boil the bones.

Most of my 1907 farmhouse was remodeled using salvaged materials from the Habitat for Humanity resale shops and scrap yards. My living room floor was a high school basketball court for over seventy years. My bathroom sinks and cast-iron tub are from a Seattle hotel that was built in the 1800s. When it was converted to modern condos, the old fixtures, faucets, sinks, and lights were ripped out and recycled. I think I bought half of the old hotel! But all that thriftiness was magnified by a million when I came face-to-face with the reality of the world.

"Live simply that others may simply live" became my life's motto, my mantra, after my first trip to Africa.

I have taken no fewer than twenty associates with me on various trips to West Africa, and a few have processed the reality of life and death in a similar way; yet few seem to have been impacted like I was and inspired to change their lives.

When you stand looking at a child's lifeless body, dead for lack of twelve dollars' worth of malaria medications, or simply for want of clean water, when you see a young boy, eight or nine years old, working in a rock quarry in the punishing sun just to earn a dollar for the pile of rocks he chips using a crude metal hammer, when you go to the country's premier hospital and witness two or three babies lying in one crib, no sheets or bedding, no clean needles for the doctors to administer an IV, you realize *very quickly* how different life in a developing nation is.

When I see a friend pull up in a new Tesla that carries an $80,000 price tag, or when I talk to another broadcaster who spends $2,000 a night for a hotel room in Vegas, I honestly feel a wrenching in my gut. It's the same physical sensation I used to experience when I would go to the Buruli Ulcer Clinic in Ghana and see the patients with limbs that were eaten away by a disease similar to leprosy. I'd have to excuse myself and go to the latrine to throw up when I'd see the young children with their flesh eaten away, lying on sheetless beds, eyes glazed from the pain.

Eight years later, I barely flinch when I visit the clinic in Ghana. Point Hope has provided bandages, wound care, nutritional support, a physical therapist, medical supplies, books, toys, and clothes for those battling this baffling tropical disease. I'm there to visit patients who have been admitted for six months or more and meet the latest arrivals diagnosed with this dreaded disease that has no known cause, and sadly, is rarely diagnosed in time to cure before limbs are badly affected. It takes many months, sometimes years, once the progression has stopped, for the ulcers to heal.

Our international director of Point Hope, Jan Haynes, visits the Buruli clinic far more often than I do. Jan is a knitter, and during one of her visits she was knitting a shawl. A few of the patients were curious as to what she was doing, so she demonstrated her skills with the needles and yarn. Interest turned to excitement, and before long, she had created a knitters' group within the clinic. Little did she know her favorite pastime would end up transforming lives! The patients spent long days, weeks, and months shut inside a small clinic made of cinder bricks. There were few family visits, no entertainment, and little to distract them from the physical and emotional pain they were experiencing. Knitting became a fun distraction, but when they realized they could sell the goods they created, it took on an entirely new meaning!

In America and Europe, knitting is considered a woman's hobby, but because there is no such framework in Africa, the male patients were intrigued as much as the women. Hats, scarves, purses, and lap blankets began to take form. Jan couldn't keep up with the demand for needles and yarn, so we started scouting thrift stores for these simple tools. We packed bags with donated or thrift store yarn and then vacuum packed them, getting dozens of skeins in a suitcase. A surprising gift came with the Buruli patients' love of knitting—the doctor in charge of the clinic reported that the men who were knitting had lower blood pressure, and as a result their wounds were able to heal much faster. Not only that, many patients had lost flesh and muscle from their hands and arms due to the virus, but the knitting forced them to use their limbs, which turned out to be an amazing form of physical therapy.

With knitting came possibilities to create things of beauty as well as generate income. With that came hope, and when hope replaced despair, the pain of the disease became much more manageable. In teaching a few people to knit, Jan impacted lives for eternity. She gave them a simple skill, which returned their dignity and gave them hope.

I live between two worlds, and it is difficult for me not to judge when I see rail-thin young women shopping at impeccably decorated upscale stores that carry designer handbags as costly as a monthly mortgage payment. My initial reaction to stories of hundred-dollar hot yoga sessions and manicures is irritation. When I see rich young music artists with diamonds in their teeth or gold grills gleaming when they flash their million-dollar smiles, or celebrities lazing around the deck of a yacht that costs more than the annual budget of an orphanage that could house five hundred homeless, hopeless refugee children, I feel frustration and despair.

I want to take them all to Africa, to see and experience the things I have. I'm just *sure* that if I could, their priorities would get straightened out. I must remind myself, however, as I learned from Tina, you can lead a horse to water, but you cannot make him drink. People must experience life on their own terms, but oh, if I can find a way to tell them my story, I will take advantage of it!

My mind now works like this: if every decision impacts a thousand different decisions, then if I decide to go into debt to buy a new car, I am deciding to spend

$500 a month on an auto payment and insurance that I could be spending on food for orphaned children. If I decide to spend $360 on a purse from Nordstrom, I am deciding not to buy $360 worth of bandage materials for Buruli ulcer patients. If I decide to go out to dinner with my husband and we ring up an eighty-dollar tab for food I could have easily prepared at home for fifteen dollars, then I am saying that sixty-five-dollar difference, which would feed two refugees for an entire month, was worth the experience.

And yet, I am no saint. I do make these decisions every day. I do not live in poverty. My older children have cell phones, an American necessity. We eat dinners out when the day or week has been overwhelmingly busy or there is a birthday or occasion to celebrate. I splurge on experiences and items I know will make my loved ones smile. But my frugality is famous, and my heart with those in need.

∽

My producer and best friend Janey has a beautiful daughter named Jesse. Because Janey was established in her career when she adopted Jess and because Jess is an only child, Janey spoiled her rotten from the day her curly head came into this world. If Jesse ordered a plate of pasta and then decided she didn't like it after one or two bites, Janey would toss it in the garbage and order a burger for her instead.

When Jess was about nine years old, Janey came to Africa with me. She walked through the Buduburam refugee camp. She went to the orphanages with me. She held sick babies and watched the mothers with hollow cheeks and vacant eyes try to comfort their daughters, weak with malnutrition as their distended bellies begged for nutrition. Janey cried like I have never seen her cry before. I believe her heart was broken as deeply as it had been when her amazing father, the pillar and rock of their family, died from complications from diabetes. She returned to America a changed woman.

Before Africa, Janey had always thought my love for gardening was a somewhat silly pastime. Once she saw the gardens in Africa that we created to grow healthy food for starving children and families, she began to change. Janey has never been a materialistic or selfish person, but once she saw what real poverty looked like, and once she realized that she could make a difference in the lives of others, her entire perspective shifted. No, she didn't sell all her possessions and join the Peace Corps, but a diametric shift occurred. Now she spends hours in her gardens; her once grass-only yard is a lush oasis of fruits, berries, and vegetables. She gives away as much as she uses for herself and Jesse. She packs up boxes of the clothes Jesse has outgrown and brings them to my farm for me to take to Africa to give to kids in the camp. She spends hours on the phone, talking to record reps and the managers of Céline Dion or Josh Groban, trying to get concert tickets to auction off for Point Hope. She wakes up determined to help feed one more child, to empower one more single mom.

Instead of spoiling Jesse, she is helping her beautiful daughter to view the world through a different lens. As a result, Jesse has become passionate about a number of issues and has gone with me to Africa, where she fell in love with the children and worked in the feeding program. She wants to go back—she cries over wounded animals and orphaned babies, and she has motivated other students in her school to get involved in service projects and to care about people outside of themselves.

Janey's trip not only changed her life, but her daughter's and untold others' as well. She had always been conservative with her finances and generous with her resources, but her focus to change the world for good has taken flight. She is living more simply so that others may simply live. Most every person on my staff embraces and embodies that theory. Many are gardeners and share the harvest with family, friends, and food banks. We rarely go to red carpet events together, but we do go thrift shopping! We are bound by a common goal of producing an amazing radio show seven nights a week, and a common belief that we can change the world.

$\sim$

We often live such busy lives that we're hard-pressed to find face time together with friends and family. We are conditioned to gain wealth and tangible items at the expense of quality time with people we love. Seems backward, doesn't it?

I believe it goes back to our relatively new culture of isolation. We work so hard to build up our respective kingdoms—for what? To be trapped inside with everything to ourselves, sitting behind a computer or phone screen, snapping photos of our worldly possessions for all of our virtual friends to see and like.

Do you want to experience true peace in your life? *Live simply.* I'm not telling you to sell all of your possessions or give them away, or move to a remote village in Africa. I'm saying be like Janey—open your eyes to the impact you can have on others by making small adjustments in your lifestyle. Get involved in your community and learn about homelessness, foster children, orphans, disabled veterans. Find a cause you care about so you too will begin to think about how your decisions impact a thousand more decisions.

The only fact we know about life is that we all die. It's also a fact that we take nothing with us when we meet our maker. I hope and pray that when we stand before Him, we can demonstrate ways we lived simply so others may simply live.

CHAPTER 8:
A WOUNDED HEART

During a third visit to the group children's home to see our potential son, Manny, his younger siblings were visiting. Manny was twelve, Tangi was eleven, and TJ was nine; Alonzo and Estina, the two youngest, were there as well. They were living with their father at the time. He had spent time in prison but fought for his kids when he was released. Manny's father was out of the picture, as was the father of Tangi and TJ. Their mother was drug addicted and led a high-risk life. They were a close-knit group of kids despite the fact they had all been in the foster care system for years. Only the two youngest had been placed together; the other three were split up over and over again. When we were sitting at the dining table about to enjoy cake, Manny looked at me and smiled his famous smile, then he looked at Tangi and TJ and said, "You take one, you take us all," and I knew he meant it in his tender heart. He was letting me know the bond they shared was not to be broken even if we adopted him.

A few weeks after our first visit, we were able to take Manny home on the weekends but had to return him to the group home each Sunday evening so he could finish out the school year. It was a lot of driving for no reason, as he did not have a passing grade in any of his classes. My new son had been placed in eleven different foster homes during his time in the system.

Each time a foster child is placed with a new family and then removed, their ability to form healthy bonds with other humans is damaged. After two or three removals and reassignments, their hearts shut down and stop trying. Consistency is not a factor in the life of a child taken by the state. The only thing that remains consistent is their daily fear of everything in their lives. Fear that they will not see their biological parent again, fear that they will be moved to an abusive home, fear that they won't be removed when they are abused. Fear that they won't fit in at school, fear that they will come home from school and be expected to interact at a dinner with a family they know nothing about. They fear coming home to discover a case worker's car in the driveway and their few possessions crammed in garbage bags as they get dragged to another placement.

If you want to have your heart broken into a million pieces, spend a few hours at your local library learning about the state of foster care in our country. In a country obsessed with safety concerns for children, wonderful car-seat technology, product warnings and recalls on toys, it amazes me that so many children are routinely physically, emotionally, and sexually abused in our foster care system, and no one says a word. Most children in foster care are born and raised in poverty. Most have a mother or father that has a history of addiction and/or mental illness. Most enter the system already scarred and scared...

Manny and Sonny moved upstairs into a room under the eaves that ran the length of the house. Our roommate and my producer, Janey, had a stuffy front room upstairs. Baby Shaylah was on the main floor with my husband and I. Manny's younger siblings, Tangi and TJ, often visited on the weekends and school breaks. Six people, sometimes eight, now lived in a three-bedroom house with only one bathroom. It was getting cozy.

Sonny and Manny quickly discovered their mutual love for soccer. They laughed, joked, and played as if they had known each other their entire lives, and I only saw them fight one time. Sonny was tall and thin as a rail; he was prone to shyness and very even tempered. Manny was short and chubby, had an outgoing personality, and was prone to fly into fits of anger with little provocation. Sonny had long legs and ran like a gazelle; Manny was a powerhouse. They made a great team on and off the soccer field.

In August of 1998 I decided to take the kids camping. I invited Tangi and TJ to come along, and their case worker approved the trip. We planned the trip and packed tents, blankets, ice coolers, and swimsuits. I packed Shay's nebulizer and extra batteries in case it failed. We were armed with EpiPens and Benadryl, bug spray and citronella candles to keep the mosquitoes away from her. We joined my sister DeAnna's family in a national park for the Labor Day weekend.

Shay's health was good, and she didn't have any asthma flare-ups. Manny and Sonny got lost hiking for a bit but soon found their way back to camp. Tangi and TJ had the time of their lives climbing on trees and jumping in the river. Just one thing interrupted the serenity of the camping trip for me—a secret I was carrying. Literally.

A few days before we left on the camping trip, I was feeling queasy and had a headache. I was a few days late... On my way to a soccer tournament with the boys and Shay in the back of my mom's old van, I stopped at a store for Gatorade, snacks, cheese sticks, bottled water, and a pregnancy test.

During halftime I had the boys watch their little sister, and I went into the ladies' room. Standing in the stall I stared in disbelief as the little plus sign formed in the window. I was pregnant.

I stuck the test back in the foil pouch, back in the cardboard box and into my purse. I was pregnant. I was pregnant with a husband I had been separated from twice and felt little connection to; pregnant despite the fact doctors told me it was not possible; pregnant despite the fact I was using birth control after we decided to adopt Manny. I was pregnant and expecting a baby at almost forty.

I was lost in thought during the camping trip; the drive to the mountain park was long and I kept getting carsick. By the time we arrived and started to unpack, I was exhausted and dehydrated. But the kids were excited and kept climbing on logs and trees and wanted to jump in the stream. We got the huge family-size tent set up, the

My arrival—February 15, 1960.
Held by my father.

An early family portrait with my parents and brother,
Matthew—sixteen months older than me.

Matt and me with my grandmother, Eula McGowne
(Gramma Mac). She was a huge influence in my life.

Our pet sheep, Robie Dobie, who used to pull me
around in a cart. I have always LOVED animals!

This is the old rented farmhouse we lived in until I was ten.
My parents repaired the old lathe and plaster walls by
mixing oatmeal into paint. They also painted the outside.
I have such fond memories of this house.

A birthday gathering for my grandfather, Bud McGowne
(Grammpa Mac). It's a rare photo with my mom in it, as she
was usually taking the pictures. Gramma and my siblings, Matt,
DeAnna, and Timothy too.

Another birthday celebration. Gramma Mac always
brought a gift for everyone.

Me on "Old Joe." My equine love
started at a young age.

KDUN, the voice of Dune Country. My first radio job, in Reedsport, Oregon.

The only family portrait we have, from a free sitting I won in 1978, the year I graduated high school. DeAnna, Matthew, and me in back; Timothy and Dad second row; Mom in front.

My parents in June of 1982.

Our last sibling gathering before we lost Matt and Anne in the plane crash. Everyone came to Seattle to visit in August 1984. I was eight months pregnant with Isaiah (Sonny). Tim, me, DeAnna, Anne, and Matt.

Gramma Mac, me, and Mom holding her first grandchild, Isaiah, who was almost immediately known as Sonny, a nickname his dad gave him.

Hosting the New Year's Eve celebration at the Space Needle, Seattle—December 31, 1985.

Robin Hood and Maid Marian (Sonny and me).
At this point I was a single mother living in Boston.

Sonny and me in Boston in 1991, spending time with friends.

Now a single mother of eight! Isaiah, Emmanuelle, and Trey in back. Zachariah, me, Shaylah, and Tanginique in front. Thomas K on my lap.

Mercy and Willette in Buduburam, Ghana, who became my daughters, Angel and Blessing, in the US.

Sonny's graduation from the Police
Academy. Fortunately his father,
George Harris, was able to attend.

The snow adventure that preceded the invitation to The African
Children's Choir to join us for lunch at the farm. Shaylah, me,
Thomas, my granddaughter Jayla, and our host, Zachariah.

My Bridget and Sammy in Ghana, before I brought them home to their forever family.

Sammy at home with me, Mama Bear, and his forever family in the US.

Gathering water with the children in Ghana.

Jan ("Mama Jan") Haynes, our executive
director of Point Hope.

Children being fed in the Point Hope Nutrition Project.

A few members of my family in Sammy's garden—my therapy as I grieved for him, and a monument to his life.

My "person," executive director of the *Delilah*
radio program, Jane Bulman.

My siblings today: DeAnna, me, and Tim.
Always by my side.

National Radio Hall of Fame induction, Chicago, November 2016.
With niece Laurel and daughters Lonika and Shaylah (on left),
husband Paul, and siblings DeAnna and Tim (on right). So blessed!

My induction into the NAB Hall of Fame—Las Vegas, April 2017.
Doubly blessed!

My precious son, Zachariah Miguel Rene-Ortega.

sleeping bags rolled out, the coolers unpacked, and the hot dogs roasted. I had not told anyone except my husband, my best friend, Janey, and my sister, DeAnna, and I still was not sure how I felt about my condition. I was happy—I loved being a mom above all else—but this unexpected surprise threw me for a total loop.

That night, after the kids settled into their sleeping bags and the lanterns were turned off, I started to tell stories and sing silly songs to the children sleeping in the tent. It was our tradition, and no amount of exhaustion on my part would satisfy their enthusiasm. Finally they began to nod off, one by one.

Sometime after midnight when the entire campground had settled down and the sounds of the mountain forest at night began to lull me to sleep, I heard a voice in the dark and felt a small hand reach for mine. It was Manny's younger brother, TJ. He grabbed my hand and asked if I was asleep. When I said no, I was just about to doze off, he said, "Can I call you Mom, like Manny does?" Then I heard sobbing and a final statement: "'Cause I don't have a mom anymore and I want to call you my mom."

I couldn't stop the tears from choking my voice, whether it was my pregnancy hormones or just pure love, I reached out to cradle his head in my arms and soothe him and replied, "Of course. You can call me Mom or Mama. I answer to both."

There was one defining event in my life that changed the course of my life forever… it was more of a project than an event, but it was one of those things that probably rearranged the DNA chain in my being, and has remained guiding me to this day.

I was in Mrs. Lyons's fourth-grade class, my first year in Reedsport after moving from the farm up Coos River. I wasn't exactly excited to start at the new school, and I wasn't exactly popular. The school I left behind had a total of thirteen kids in my grade; this new school had *four* classes of fourth graders, almost one hundred students. As God would have it, I was put in Mrs. Lyons's class, which was an amazing miracle. Not just because she loved reading and allowed us to read at our own rate and move ahead several class levels, and not just because she was an educated, strong woman who encouraged all her students, boys as well as girls, to exceed our own expectations and to always do our best. No. The best part of being is Mrs. Lyons's fourth grade class was the fact that her son, Bill, had served in Vietnam.

I spoke with Mrs. Lyons recently about the project we did in her class, and even though she's in her eighties now, her memories of the Vietnam project were as clear as they were over forty years ago when she introduced us to the concept of giving to those in desperate need. Her son eventually retired after spending twenty-two years in the US Army, and today he's a groundskeeper for the golf course in our hometown.

When Bill's mission in Vietnam was complete, he stayed behind. There were villages that had been decimated by the Viet Cong farther north of his station; the men were conscripted into serving in the military, and the adult women had been taken and used in the sex trade.

All that was left of some of the villages were the elderly and children. Bill Lyons's heart broke for these children, and along with some Catholic nuns, he did all that he could to ensure they would live and be cared for.

The year was 1970 when Bill, in his late twenties, wrote to his mother about one particular village and the utter despair he witnessed in the orphanage. She brought her son's letters to school and read them to our class. We sat in awed silence, twenty-two usually noisy, fidgety nine- and ten-year-olds. When she finished reading his neat handwriting, tears were in her eyes and streaming down our faces. Even Billy Town, the biggest kid in our school, was visibly touched.

The conditions Bill described were heartbreaking: orphans with no clothes, no shoes, no blankets, lying on their mats when they went to sleep at night.

With Mrs. Lyons's direction, we wrote dozens of ideas on the chalkboard about ways we could help. Because reading and education was so important to her, she encouraged us to collect storybooks in good shape and bring them in. She invited us to bring in used clothes, and when we did, she inspected each garment. If there was a tear, she taught us how to mend it. If there was a button missing, she searched through her own button can and taught us how to sew one back on that matched as closely as possible. We paired socks, mended hems, sewed patches on jeans.

Our teacher brought in her ironing board and taught all of us how to iron, starting with pillowcases and towels, and graduating to dresses and slacks. We gladly gave up our lunch hours and recesses; even the boys took a turn at the ironing board and tried to one-up each other with the creases in their discarded slacks. Our camaraderie and purpose were palatable. The enthusiasm spread to other classes, and soon the entire fourth grade was working together to collect pens and pencils, books and paper, blankets and shoes and plenty of socks.

I came home from school excited to raid our closets. Our home was well organized, and clothes were always mended and handed down; there was only one set of sheets per twin bed, and I think we used the same four or five bath towels for ten years until they were threadbare. But we were far better off than the almond-eyed children staring blankly in the Polaroid photos Bill Lyons had mailed us from the orphanage in Vietnam.

Dad came home one day to find me raiding the junk drawer in the kitchen that held pencils, pens, rubber bands, and bread-bag twists. I had bundled up a handful of pencils, wound a rubber band around them to donate, and Dad questioned why I was taking them. I eagerly told him about our project, how we were even collecting pop cans to redeem for the five-cent return fee that was part of Oregon's recycling project so we could pay the shipping fees. I fully expected him to embrace the project and hand over his coveted red engineering pencils. Like so many other times I thought he would be proud of something I had embarked upon or an idea I embraced, his mood turned dark and angry; he demanded to know whose idea it was. I stammered and told him about Mrs. Lyons's son, Bill, who had stayed behind in Vietnam to help the orphans, and how they had nothing and no one to care for them. The more I talked, the angrier he became.

"You will not participate in this asinine project," he barked and then launched into one of his lectures about how they would have killed our soldiers if they had a chance, and on and on and on. Dejected and heartbroken, I went to my room and considered my options—disobey and get my butt beat if I got caught, or do what I wanted to do and help kids who had no one to care for them. The choice was pretty simple. I stuffed the items I'd pilfered from the house in my book bag or layered them under my own clothes and shed them in the girl's bathroom. Lunch hours and recesses were spent washing, ironing, folding, hemming, and stepping on collected pop cans to take to the recycling center. Each student involved wrote a letter to the children, and Bill Lyons promised to have them translated for us.

As the project grew and the boxes were packed, the local newspaper decided to visit our class and write a story. My show-off gene took over, completely silencing the be-wise-and-don't-get-caught thought that quickly fluttered out of my mind. Being the tallest girl in the class, my smiling face beamed out from the middle of the photo at least five inches above the other girls who were crowded in. As I recall we stood behind the ironing board, holding donated items.

Dad was mad, but for some reason I didn't get the expected punishment. The enthusiasm and passion that project fueled has only grown over the years. I heard a speaker at a retreat share that in the process of doing any-thing, the final outcome is not what is important—the relationships formed during the event are what really mat-ters. Looking back, that project forged relationships and memories that last to this day, over four decades later. But it was also a definitive project that showed us we could make a difference in our world, we could impact the world for good, we could change the life of a child who was cold, barefoot, and alone. We could reach out in love and change the world, one heart at a time.

I started Point Hope and found local people to work with me and help those who are most vulnerable. And just like Mrs. Lyons, today I have my kids and teachers in our small community collecting used clothes, shoes, sheets, and school tools that we ship to West Africa to help kids who have no one else to advocate for them. With the exception of ironing the slacks and pressing a crease, we set up a staging area in my living room for a month prior to my trips twice a year, and the kids pack suitcases and boxes just like we did at Highland Elementary School in Mrs. Lyons's class.

If I had the power to do so, I would replicate Mrs. Lyons's project and make it part of the standard curriculum in every fourth-grade class across America. I know a lot of classes already do this sort of thing, and conversely, I know other classes could use this sort of blessing. I would love to see kids helping other kids, whether it's gathering resources for other underprivileged schools, foster children, or orphans abroad.

Can you imagine the change we could effect in our country if young minds were tuned in and turned on to helping others who aren't just like them? Who don't look like them or live like them? I think we tend to want to shelter our kids from these worldly problems, and this was more than likely why my dad forbade me to participate, but I really believe if we could gently break their hearts to the things that break God's, we would be setting them up for a lifetime of compassion and action. Rather than talking or protesting about inequality on social media, our children would get up in the morning and be the ones to make something happen that betters their communities.

Let's get back to what you can do right now—kids or no kids. If your eyes are on this book, and you've gotten this far, your heart is in the right place. You want to spread more love in this world. Deep down you know too many kids go hungry, too many kids are abused, too many kids wish for a safe person they can call Mommy or Daddy and a stable home where they can lay their heads at night. There are hundreds of thousands of children who will go to sleep tonight not knowing if they will have a forever home. Let it sink in.

When you open your cupboards or your pantry to graze over the ingredients for the makings of a filling lunch or dinner, think of the child who has no choice but to go hungry. Think how crazy it makes you to be hungry when you're trying to get work done, and now consider the child who has to go to school hungry. Think of all the belongings you own that you've collected over the years, and now think of the child whose whole world can fit into a garbage sack. Think of the kisses you give your loved ones at night or the embrace you give before sending them off in the morning... and think of the little child whose only touch is the harsh hand of an abusive guardian. Let it break your heart.

I understand not everyone can be a foster parent, but I believe with my whole heart everyone can help a child in need. Make a personal sacrifice to help a child. Give up your daily latte and use those funds to help a child in need. Much to the disappointment of my kids, I don't usually go in for the flash of new cars, or grown-up toys many think I could afford because of my radio career success. It's because my joy is found in relationships, the land, and critters. It's because I love, love, *love* feeding kids who are hungry. I love, love, *love* providing skills training for impoverished women. I love, love, *love* knowing I can make a difference in people's lives.

Generations ago people were dependent upon the help of their neighbor, and willing to assist others, so that they would have someone to turn to when they needed it. Whether it was lending a hand or a machine during harvesttime, a barn raising, getting a wounded person to a doctor, or sharing fruits and vegetables with those who did not have any gardens, neighbors helped neighbors. Sadly, our culture has gone the opposite direction. Not only do we *not* reach out to those in need, but in an attempt to protect them, we teach our children to mind their own business and to look away when they see something that's displeasing or heartbreaking.

Evidence of this mentality is everywhere. Many years ago, my sister worked for a shoe store that was part of a large national chain. If anybody returned a pair of shoes because they did not fit, those shoes could not be resold. Instead of donating them to homeless people or children who lived in poverty, the store employees were trained to take a box cutter and destroy the shoes, then throw them in the trash. The manager explained the chain did not want their unsold or damaged shoes ending up at garage sales or thrift stores so that they could be returned to the store for cash. I wonder, how often would that have happened? Would the chain really lose so many profits?

Last year I walked into a bakery and asked what they did with their day-old bread. I wanted to collect it to give to our local food bank. The manager of the bakery explained they put the day-old bread in a locked dumpster each night. They did not want to donate it for those who might be hungry because they did not want to be liable for any health issues. Instead they locked it up in the trash so no one, not even a farmer's pigs, could benefit from it.

Policies and rules have become far more important than stepping in to help when there is a real need. I've heard of people who were afraid to perform CPR out of fear they would be held accountable if a person did not survive. So they stood by and watched, hoping someone else would provide aid, rather than perform a lifesaving service. How confined in our little safe zones we have become, while the devil laughs louder.

We need more communities helping each other; we need more teachable moments. If you have a child in your care or a young person you can influence, I encourage you to get them involved in service projects, and talk to them about why you do it. After a holiday or a birthday, for each new toy a child receives, you could ask them to pick out an old toy to donate to a child in need. Every time a child grows out of their school clothes, you can show them some choices for where their old clothes could benefit other children. You could make sandwiches for a tent city or a homeless shelter, and let the younger generation be a part of this compassion project. My policies and rules for helping the needy come from the Bible—I think we should all consult this operations guide more often.

CHAPTER 9:
A HEART REDEEMED

I didn't have a clue why I experienced the painful things I did growing up, why I was born with slightly deformed legs that led to clumsy casts and bulky leg braces. All I knew was that I was insecure about my own body and subject to bullying for it. Now when I see a child with a disability or impairment, my compassion for them and my desire to bless them is heightened. Would I feel that way had I not tried to run as a child, stumbling and falling with the steel braces strapped to my legs? I'll never know.

When I first started going to West Africa, I met a few children who had lost limbs in the Liberian and Sierra Leonean civil wars, but there was an absence of kids with special needs at the refugee camp to which they had fled. I noticed kids who were starving and dying from malaria, and the small clinic was overflowing with children who had cholera, dysentery, and tropical diseases. But they were otherwise typical children. I rarely saw any with physical deformities, Down syndrome, mental retardation, cerebral palsy... where were the children who were blind or hearing impaired? Or ones who needed braces as I did on my legs?

It wasn't until my second year of work in Ghana that I began to understand the answers to these questions. It was not me, but a French volunteer who had come to work as the hospital administrator, Sebastian Nerault, and his lovely wife, Ellise, who made the discovery. Ellise's educational background was in special needs education and physical therapy. She too noticed an absence of children with typical special needs in the eighty-thousand-plus population of immigrants from war-torn countries. She began to inquire and found her way to a woman named Elisabeth, who had started a small program for special-needs children within the camp. She shared with us which families had mentally or physically disabled kids. Their superstitions dictated these children were cursed or possessed, and as a result, they kept their children hidden from view, locked away in minuscule mud huts, where they could not be judged or abused.

Ellise went door to door, knocking and asking if a child was there who needed help. She spent two years earning the trust of the refugees and assuring them she could help their children, not bring them harm.

She worked with Elisabeth to establish Harmony Center, an educational program for children and young adults with special needs and disabilities. They met in a small classroom and used their meager resources to try to educate and work with children who not only had profound special needs, but who had never been socialized, never had exercise, and never met others outside their small compound or neighborhood.

Sebastian and Ellise finished their volunteer term and returned to France. Elisabeth contacted me and asked if Point Hope would sponsor this project. I went to their small room and sat and watched kids come to life. Children who had never been off the woven mats on the floor of their huts were learning to sit in wooden chairs; some were learning to crawl or walk. I stifled tears as they showed the songs they had learned to sing, as they waved atrophied limbs in the air and clapped to "If You're Happy and You Know It, Clap Your Hands." When one young girl with cerebral palsy, who had never walked or even crawled, scooted across the cement floor to climb in my lap, the tears would not stay hidden behind my glasses. They ran down my face, and then I found myself sobbing as I rocked her. I could clearly see why God had allowed the braces on my crooked legs, why I endured the taunts of "clod-hoppers" from classmates. I could relate in a teeny-tiny way to the pain each child had faced, being locked away out of shame, fear, or spiritual superstitions. I had experienced feeling awkward and clumsy, but these children had experienced feeling unwanted, unloved, and even being persecuted for a perceived evil that had befallen their family and cursed their body.

For over a decade, Harmony Center was the only known program established by refugees for the education and betterment of disabled and special-needs children. Elisabeth and other volunteers have saved countless lives and given hundreds of children with disabilities dignity and hope.

Point Hope has partnered with the Harmony Center from the moment I sat in their small, dark, cramped classroom. First, we provided a much bigger and nicer classroom for the students and volunteers, then an entire section of a school building, adjacent to the school and feeding program we ran. But to illustrate how ingrained the prejudice and ignorance was about these children in the culture, previously, we had built a playground within the same complex. A retired Ghanaian physician oversaw the Point Hope nutrition program and early-intervention day care, which shared the same space with Harmony. I discovered the physician and his nurses were not allowing the Harmony students to play on the playground equipment we had provided, nor were the students allowed to use the indoor toilets at the school complex. It was an irrational fear of touching or being near the Harmony kids, a belief that they were somehow unclean—a conviction the doctor, the nurses, the teachers, and the parents were clinging to.

Point Hope's director, Jan, gently tried to change the environment—she knew when I showed up and found out what was going on, it wouldn't be good. She was right. I threw a nutty and by the time the dust settled, everyone understood if Point Hope was going to fund the school, pay the teachers' salaries, and buy the food for the nutrition program, they *would* work hard to make the Harmony kids feel welcomed and loved. Together, Jan and Elisabeth began integrating the special-needs students into the regular routine of the school whenever possible, until the Harmony kids and our other students saw nothing unusual about sharing the space, including the playground and restrooms.

Jan Haynes had embraced the Harmony program from her first trip to Ghana and searched for new and better ways to provide for the needs of the students. When in America, both Jan and I continually searched thrift stores and garage sales for wheelchairs, crutches, scooters, exercise balls, and other items to be used for very basic physical therapy, as well as used eyeglasses and books about sign language and Braille to schlep back to Africa.

Once again, God intervened. Joe Worthington, a licensed practical nurse from Wyoming, had traveled to Ghana planning to volunteer at the clinic in the camp. He had received some training in physical therapy during his schooling and agreed to work with Elisabeth and the Harmony program. He discovered a passion for special-needs kids. Joe was a miracle worker. Kids with cerebral palsy who could not walk or crawl, after working with Joe and the few tools he collected, learned not only to crawl, but actually to walk. He taught mothers how to use rubber tubing to exercise their children's legs and arms, how to use simple plastic toys to motivate kids to try to pick things up, developing fine motor skills. He extended his volunteer assignment for another two years and asked Point Hope to provide a massage table so he could work with each child, teaching their parents to massage their atrophied limbs. Joe also built a rudimentary wooden apparatus with low parallel bars just the right size for toddlers to hold on to. He inspired crippled kids to hold on to the bars and take one small step. Then two. Three... down and back! Again, I fought back tears as I watched Joe pour his heart into these kids and into their moms and dads—parents, who in turn showed other parents with special-needs kids they could bring their children out into the light and into the care of this kind man.

Now, with the help of many volunteers, and working to change the culture of the Buduburam community through education, the Harmony children have been integrated into the Ghana public education system in a primary school we donated.

Point Hope has also partnered with PETS International, a volunteer organization in the US that builds wooden personal energy transportation (PET) carts, which are pedaled by hand, so people who don't have use of their legs can still be mobile and even run a micro business using their carts. To date, we have shipped and helped to distribute about four hundred carts across Ghana. To see these people who otherwise would be hopeless hand-pedaling their carts and selling food and provisions from the ample trunk built in the design is a thrill beyond measure.

As for the Harmony Center kids like Princess, Magda, Elsa, Kofi, Stephen, and everyone there working with them, they are thriving! Each trip back I try to take hand weights or an exercise mat, an inflatable yoga ball or jump ropes. Simple tools, but priceless in the physical and mental development of dozens of kids who were labeled possessed and demonized. Now they run, laugh, sing, read, talk in sign language to classmates who can hear, and use their wheelchairs or crutches to maneuver the streets and pathways. Point Hope worked with Elisabeth as she taught crafting skills, creating goods the older teens and young adults could produce and sell. She taught them sound business practices and how to market their beautiful creations. They are learning to be world citizens.

And I have to believe that the chubby little girl who fell jumping across a mud puddle up Coos River while wearing steel braces on her legs was being prepared to love on these children who couldn't jump across a puddle, either.

Dad had charged me room and board the last few years of high school. His reasoning was that I was earning an income at KDUN, the radio station, and I needed to help contribute to the household expenses. A ridiculous notion to me, and one I resented deeply. Today I thank God for the lessons I learned about being financially accountable and paying my own way through life. I've never expected or depended upon another person to pay my bills. I learned early that you do *not* buy luxury items or things to please yourself if you owe money to someone else, and to never owe money to someone else! Mom and Dad did not use credit except to buy our eighteen-hundred-square-foot family home.

When friends and peers bought new cars, skis, motorcycles, hot tubs, Hawaiian vacations, designer heels and bags with their credit cards, I ate Top Ramen, bought clothing and household goods at thrift stores, and drove used cars that I purchased at auctions. I had a roommate in college named Suzie who was on public assistance and received financial aid for school. She spent the cash she was able to come by on weed and booze and other self-gratifying purchases. I was so frustrated when she used her food stamps at the grocery store, knowing she'd picked up a case of beer just an hour before.

Dad told me once, when I was about thirteen and making fifty cents an hour babysitting, "Sis, don't ever use credit or go into debt. If you go into debt, you owe the man. If you owe the man, you have to work, no matter how much you hate your job. If you want to quit, you can't because you have too many bills you have to pay. But if you never go into debt, you can tell the man to kiss my ass and walk out the door." Best. Lesson. Ever.

Fortunately, the same principle applied to getting fired, which was good, because I got fired a lot. But Dad's financial education and my somewhat obsessive work ethic allowed me to buy my first house at twenty-one, my second at twenty-six, and my third at thirty. If there is one piece of advice I would give to every young person, it would be the same as Dad told me. Don't ever go into debt or use credit. When you agree to buy something you can't afford, you may think you are getting an amazing thing in the short run, but in the long run you are giving up your freedom to say "kiss my ass."

Mom also taught me financial wisdom, but by different means. She married young, at nineteen, to a charismatic blue-eyed man, and agreed to stay home, be a wife, and raise kids while he worked to support the family. By giving up her options to have a job or career, she gave up everything. My dad controlled her and her purse strings as well as her choices, her options, and her freedom. My father even shopped for my mother's clothes. He once spotted a polyester pantsuit from a flimsy mail catalog, and since the suit came in tall, he ordered two of them, blue and gold. Any time she had an occasion, my mother wore one of these two pantsuits, for years and years and years. Most of her other clothing were gifts from her parents or she made herself.

My dad decided what appliances we would have, and if they needed service he decided when, or if, he would fix them. My dad made every single decision in our family. My mom had no voice whatsoever, except of which food acceptable to Dad's palate she would make for dinner. We were fortunate in the fact that our grandparents owned a small farm and grew most of our food, including the beef that we ate, but my mother still needed to do the weekly shopping for bread, milk, and staples. She was a good and thrifty shopper who always cut coupons and looked for bargains. But if she came home and she had exceeded her weekly grocery budget, my father would take the ticker-tape receipt from the grocery store and go over each one of her purchases, questioning her about every dime she spent. If she had purchased something he did not agree with, he would circle it in red. Then he would subtract the amount of all the items in red from the next week's allowance.

Mom was extremely resourceful and talented. She took an upholstery course, with my dad's permission, from the college extension program and set up a shop in our family room; even this money was expected to be turned over to my father. Since Mom had no financial independence, she looked often to her children to give her money. Actually, *give* is not the word—Mom would take our money. It became an unspoken game that we never talked about. I would put my babysitting money on the left-hand side of my top drawer beneath my socks. If I earned ten dollars, I might find two or three dollars missing by the end of the week. It must have been so shaming for her. She had no cash available and had to resort to stealing from her children. My brother, my sister, and I would discuss this behind closed doors. We came up with a way to hold on to some of our money without embarrassing our mother. If I earned ten dollars, I would put some of it in my sock drawer, knowing that Mom would take two or three, and the rest I would squirrel away in an old black leather purse hidden in my closet.

When I got a little older and my father asked me to pay room and board, I did the same thing. He asked that I pay half of my income, so I lied. If I earned $200 in a month, I would tell him I earned a hundred dollars and give him fifty. I'd put the other fifty in my bank account. And the rest I would hide in the old black leather purse.

One day Mom was sitting at her sewing machine working on some upholstery when she began talking to me about financial independence. She said, "Sis, you and your sister are smart and you're beautiful, but please don't get married and have children when you are young. If you do, you'll have to depend upon your husband to support you, and you'll end up in the same mess I'm in."

Over and over and over she drilled into my head that I should never be dependent upon a man, because to do so means you give up your freedom. I have always been fiercely independent—I was born that way. So when I took my father's commandments about not being in debt and married them with my mother's commandments about not being dependent upon a husband, I made up my mind that I would always be able to take care of myself.

I judged my mother harshly when I was a young woman, because I didn't understand why she wouldn't just leave my father. She was smart, strong, and capable. I believed she could have easily gotten a job and supported herself. When I got a little older and a little wiser, I realized my mother did not view herself as others viewed her. Where we saw her as strong and beautiful, she saw herself as awkward and clumsy. Where I saw her as talented and creative, she saw herself as uneducated and ignorant; it was a combination of the times, the stigma of her Ozark background, and self-esteem issues. She always felt the need to apologize for just being who she was and always felt somewhat awkward in social settings.

Sadly, I see this in my sister, too. DeAnna is strong, beautiful, and far smarter than I will ever be, but she doesn't view herself in that light; she always feels that she's just not quite *enough*. And now I have a young adult daughter who is the same way. It must be genetic, this trait that my grandmother passed to my mother and my mother to my sister. It somehow missed me, but it passed through to my daughter. All four, stunningly beautiful women, are differently gifted but ingenious, and none see themselves in that way.

And then there is me. My sister, DeAnna, said to me one time that it didn't matter whether I was having a million-dollar day or looked and felt like dog poop, "You always act like you look beautiful and other people always believe you!" And it is true. Beauty isn't just in the eye of the beholder, beauty is about how you project yourself. If you feel beautiful, powerful, and strong, that is what people see, even if you aren't a fashion model or as perfect as the airbrushed women on the cover of magazines.

The night I graduated high school, in June of 1978, I'd already saved over $5,000, hidden in the old purse. I felt liberated! I had a good job making $3.50 an hour in radio and I owned my own car free and clear. It was an old green Pinto purchased at a state surplus auction for $500. I was dating a handsome, blond young man named Jim, and I was on top of the world. I thought I was the queen bee and felt like nothing would stop me or slow me down. Little did I know I was barely living above poverty level, and it wasn't until many class reunions had come and gone that I realized how my folks had struggled financially.

The past fifteen years I've enjoyed financial success, but even before I signed a lucrative contract with my current syndicator I never knew I wasn't wealthy, because I applied the rules my folks had taught me. I never used credit cards, I never went in debt, and I never became dependent upon another person. Those rules, coupled with the thriftiness that I learned from my parents and grandparents who had lived during the Great Depression, made me feel quite rich.

$$\infty$$

All too often I speak with people who mourn their past. And I get it. My past wasn't full of rainbows and unicorns. I wasn't served up opportunities on a silver platter. (In fact, any silver platters I've ever had, I found for a bargain price at a thrift store or garage sale.) I can't deny or reject the hard times in my past, because they shaped me into the person I am today. And I don't think it does any good to yearn for different memories. Why look back and wish for something different? You're not going that way. That's why the windshield is wide-open and the rearview mirror is small, my friend. Because what's behind us doesn't matter nearly as much as what's in front of us.

I had braces on my legs during the most impressionable years of my youth. Because of that, I developed a thick skin for criticism, a sharp tongue that bites back at bullies, and a compassionate heart for people who suffer from disabilities. I call that a win. I firmly believe God had a plan for that gawky tween with leg braces to grow up a strong defender of disabled children who have no voice or resources to help themselves.

I could be bitter I had to pay my parents to live under their roof while still just a youth. I could be mad that my mom stole my cash. At the time, I was resentful, believe me! Do you know the adventures I could've had with that extra money? But today, I am a grateful woman for those lessons. They were harsh at the time, but they turned me into a resourceful, frugal, independent person—capable of making it as a single mother who can dress up Top Ramen a hundred different ways.

Have you ever considered that the hurts in your past are meant for something greater than you? God hurts with you. He didn't, nor doesn't, want bad things to happen to you. But here's the really interesting fact: God can redeem *anything*, and *anyone* at *any time*. Your pain and suffering of the past can be healed, and not only that, it can be used to heal others. Have you ever stopped to consider how someone else may *need* your story? That's exactly the point of this book, in case you forgot. Changing the world one heart, one story at a time. That means you telling your story of redemption and offering hope to the next person going through some tough stuff.

If you're feeling crushed by the weight of your past, by abuse, by guilt, by shame, by something you've wasted good years on, you need to ask God to redeem your pain and use it for good. Don't spend another moment feeling sorry for yourself, because you are stronger than you think. I know it. God knows it. It's time for you to take that heavy brick off your shoulders and use it to lay a firm foundation for your future.

CHAPTER 10:
A HEART THAT EMBRACES

I held on to the handrail, wearily walking up the stairs from my basement studio to the kitchen. I had been busy all day with chores around the farm, taking care of kids, and then five hours in the studio doing my nightly radio show. I was tired, looking forward to a cup of herbal tea and clean sheets on my bed. I was looking forward to sprawling out on the bed with my schnauzer, Sophia, and getting some rest. I anticipated finding a sink with a dozen dirty cups and glasses, maybe a greasy bowl with popcorn kernels and butter stuck to the bottom, and a teenager putting homework in a backpack.

Instead I was greeted with a cheery "Mom?" and the smiling face of my daughter Blessing. I have learned over the years to have a very discerning ear when it comes to inflection and enunciation. I can tell when a listener says, "I'm good" if they really are good, or if they are calling because their marriage or their life is falling apart. And I am even more adept at discerning what is about to come each time I hear, "Mom," "Mama Bear," or the shortened version "Ma-bear." If the child has a slight lift in her voice on the final syllable, then a question is about to come that may or may not require a resounding no. If there is a higher uptick at the end, I know I am about to be manipulated with big eyes and a sweet smile. If the final *M* of "Mom" drops down or ends in a quiet tone, I suspect it's confession session time and I am about to hear something I would rather not have known about.

This particular "Mom" had a definite uplift at the end, punctuated by huge brown eyes, wide-open in their pleading expression. I steeled myself for the question, knowing I was about to be asked something by a professional argument winner. Blessing had just turned twelve, but her maturity level was far beyond her actual years. And when it came to getting her way, she had studied hard under the tutelage of her older sister, Shaylah. Shay was and is the master charmer. Blessing had determined by the time she was five or six that she would *not* follow in her sister Angel's footsteps when it came to trying to sway my opinion or decision through confrontation and argument.

Angel comes out swinging. Her method of approaching any topic with me was to demand her way and then argue for hours until I either left the conversation angry and frustrated or relented out of sheer exhaustion. Blessing took mental notes and decided to try Shaylah's approach—come in soft, be charming, adorable, and prepared with facts to back up the request. And if all fails and my answer is no, relent gracefully (if not a bit sullen and silent), because I still may be apt to change my mind.

Blessing is the very essence of her name. She shows no scars from her first few years as a malnourished child born on a rusted bed held up by rocks in the dirt-floored clinic of a refugee camp. Despite the trauma, abuse, and lack of food in her toddler years, my daughter is brilliant, well adjusted, and beautiful. She's also a tad bit cunning and prone to figuring out how to get her way. This particular night she poured on the charm, and I was so exhausted I didn't even see it coming.

"Mom? Um… I was wondering if we could get an exchange student again, like Fiona and Jackson?"

In previous years, we'd hosted foreign exchange students for six to eight weeks during summer break. Our first student, Jackson, was a terribly shy thirteen-year-old from China. His father was a successful businessman and wanted Jackson to learn English so he could succeed in his academic studies. He was shy and prone to homesickness, but a sweet boy who loved pizza and fried rice. Angel was about the same age and had herself only been in America a year when Jackson arrived. The two became fast friends, and the tears flowed like rain when it was time for him to return home.

The following year the same woman at our church who had arranged Jackson's stay with us asked me to host another child, this time a young Chinese girl, Fiona. At fifteen, with a broad smile and musical laugh, Fiona was delightful. She fit into our family and learned English quickly. It was Shaylah who bonded with Fiona—both were going through that awkward teenage stage and both loved the same Disney movies. For seven weeks Fiona went with our family to the beach and the mountains, played in the ponds at the farm, and fell in love with Captain Jack, Shaylah's pet bantam rooster. The three were quite a sight—Shay with long blond hair flecked golden by the summer sun, Fiona with straight jet-black hair, and tiny Captain Jack, strutting behind the two as they ran around the farm each summer day.

When it was time to take Fiona to the goodbye gathering, our entire family was sobbing like fools. We had learned about her family and traditions. Unlike Jackson, who was part of the one-child system in China, her family had been allowed two children. She missed her sibling at home but confessed they were not close like my kids. She said she felt more like a sister to my kids than she did with her brother.

I assumed it was this same exchange program that Blessing was speaking of, but I knew it was too late in the year to be a part of the program. School would be out in less than two months, and the families that agree to host are usually identified and given training much earlier in the year. I explained this to my twelve-year-old.

Her convictions were not deterred, however, and she insisted it was not too late. I gave her the name of the woman I had worked with in the past and told her to go online and look into the program. If it wasn't too late, we could consider hosting a girl for their summer program. And with that I turned out the lights and sent her to bed; she followed me up the stairs grinning.

As the next few days passed, Blessing didn't say a thing about the exchange program, and after a week I completely forgot about it. I figured she looked into the program and discovered that indeed we had come to the table too late in the season.

Two weeks later I opened my email and found a letter whose sender I didn't recognize. It began, "Dear Miss Rene, thank you for your interest in hosting an AFS student for the 2016–2017 school year. We are excited to let you know we believe we have identified a young boy from Spain..."

I reread the letter. Top to bottom. It was instructing me how to get a security background check for myself and my husband and any other person over the age of eighteen living at the farm. And if a good match was determined, our student would be arriving in August to begin his stay.

At first I thought there had been some kind of mistake, and I hit reply to inform the nice lady who sent the very enthusiastic letter that I had not in fact requested an exchange student for an entire school year. As I was typing, I remembered the conversation in the kitchen a few weeks before when I had exhaustedly capitulated and told my twelve-year-old that, yes, she could look into the exchange program *for the summer*! I had anticipated a thirteen-year-old Chinese girl spending a few weeks wading in the creek, eating popcorn and pizza, and jumping on the trampoline. Not a handsome young man from Spain!

Delilah

I walked into the kitchen holding the letter at arm's length between my thumbs and index fingers. I held it in front of Blessing, who did not understand the discontent on my face. "What?" she exclaimed.

"Read," I demanded. "Out loud."

She had no clue what I was holding, and in her very mature voice began to read, "Dear Ms. Rene, thank you for your interest in hosting an AFS student for the 2016–2017 school year. We are excited to let you know we believe we have identified a young boy from Spain that will fit well in your family dynamics."

Her eyes lit up with excitement for a few brief seconds, then she tried to mask her enthusiasm by feigning ignorance. I did my best to look stern and angry. I demanded to know when and how she filled out the application form and was incredulous that she would sign my name. "You do know forgery is an offense that can land you in jail, right?"

Her brilliant response: "It was a computer form. I didn't sign your name, I just typed it in."

After doing my best to list all the reasons we couldn't host a foreign exchange student, Blessing started parroting back all the things I have said to my kids over the years when they were frustrated or upset that others had treated them with prejudice or shunned them because they are black. "But how will the world change if people in our small town aren't exposed to diversity and different cultures? It will be good for us to practice our Spanish language skills with someone from Spain. Think how good it will be for our family to embrace a person with a completely different background." And finally, "The letter says this boy is Catholic. God must have chosen him to stay with us since we love Jesus." The God card, she pulled the God card...

Before the week was over, my husband and I had completed the background check, sent it in, and made an appointment for a home inspection. The girls took on the task of emptying out their older sister's bedroom, festooned with red-and-black flowers painted on the walls, and prepped the room to be transformed into a blue-and-brown boy's room.

In the heat of August, Antonio—Toni—arrived, and within weeks he became another child of my heart. Silly, shy, talented (he was the genie in his school's production of *Aladdin*), and smart, he adapted well to the ways of the farm, considering he came from a very progressive neighborhood in Valencia, Spain.

He went from sit-down dinners of paella with his family each evening when his father returned home around nine p.m. to crowding around the wood table at our dining nook, eating homemade applesauce and pork chops. From city streets and buses to tractors and the farm Gator. From feeding pigeons in the parks of Valencia to feeding our three-hundred-plus chickens and gathering fresh eggs each day.

I am convinced Blessing will be a great lawyer or policy maker one day—there is absolutely no way to win an argument with that child, and she always leads with her heart. As exhausted as I am taking Toni to his various projects and outings, I have to admit it has been a true blessing to our family to have him this year.

Perhaps things will be a bit more quiet next year…
Oh, who am I kidding!

It was against all odds that I became pregnant with my daughter Shaylah. I had been told by two doctors I would need medical help to conceive, as I had polycystic ovaries, and without surgery I could not become pregnant.

On one cold December day in 1993, I took nine-year-old Sonny sledding at his school. We slid down the terraced hills over and over, until the sun slipped away and the streetlights came on. "Just one more run," he begged. I agreed, and my son and I raced down on our sleds. But with the cold night air, the snow had frozen solid and was a slick sheet of ice. Our sleds flew out of control down the hill. Sonny rolled safely off and I tried to, but somehow I managed to go barreling headfirst toward a metal light pole in the middle of the field—a field that was about five acres of open land with *one* light pole. I managed to roll off right before impact, and instead of whacking my head, I hit my side. I lay on the frozen ground, fearing I had died or was about to, but too prideful to cry for help. After what seemed like a frozen eternity, I managed to stand, gather my son (I abandoned the plastic sled), and walk home. A trip to the urgent care clinic the next day revealed a black-and-blue side, two broken ribs, and a bruised kidney. Bed rest was prescribed.

Eight weeks later I became pregnant, and to this day I'm convinced the collision ruptured the stubborn cyst on my ovary. The pain was hell, but the product is pure heaven!

I didn't start to show until my fifth month, but when I did I looked like I was carrying twins or triplets. I retained so much water my feet and legs swelled up like an elephant, and I swear I could hear the water slosh as I walked. Still, I wanted to make our weekly treks for Point Hope to the park and back alleys with tuna and lemonade, wanted to visit with our homeless friends who were expecting us.

A friend of mine, Marge Latch, had joined us on several occasions, and on this particular day she offered to drive. I sat in the passenger seat, uncomfortable in my very pregnant state and happy that she had air-conditioning. We parked in downtown Philly, met two or three other volunteers who were there to help us, and started our walk, handing out the simple sandwiches and talking to friends as I waddled down the parkway toward the art museum.

On our way back to the car to go to Rittenhouse Square, Marge panicked. She had locked her keys in the car, and the heat of the day was becoming unbearable. We discussed solutions, found someone with a phone (this was 1994, before every living person had a cell phone attached to their ear), and sat down in the shade to wait for her brother to come with a second key.

As we waited, a homeless man approached us. We had given him lunch earlier, and he came to see why we were sitting together. Marge was nervous—she was a sweet woman with a very tender heart and was being cautious around this homeless man given our circumstances. I was too uncomfortable to be cautious, and I did not remember meeting him before this particular day.

I could not guess his age. He had dark skin that shone like leather on a saddle. His hands were dirty and thin, but they looked incredibly strong. He was small framed, animated, energetic, catlike with clear green eyes. But unlike the uncomfortable energy many of our street friends had from drugs, his seemed to come from within.

From his tattered backpack, he pulled out a worn black flute case. He asked, "Can I share a miracle with you?"

He started to tell us a story. He said he'd once played the flute in an orchestra, but foolish choices in life had caused him to sell his instrument and leave the orchestra. He was walking down a side street in Philly and saw a flute, just like the one he'd once owned, in the window of a pawnshop. He only had ten dollars in his pocket, and the flute was worth hundreds. He took a chance and went in. The owner eyed him suspiciously and asked what he wanted. He asked to see the flute in the window, and the owner hesitantly gave it to him to examine. The pawnshop's owner told him it was worth over a thousand dollars, but he would take $200.

Others in our group were growing restless; they could have left in their car but didn't want to abandon Marge and me. At this point, I was engrossed in the man with the sinewy fingers and the bright-green eyes.

The homeless man went on with his story. "I asked the owner if I could play it, and he said yes. I assembled the pieces, made sure the keys worked, and started to play. When I finished my song, he said I could buy it for however much money I had on me. I gave him the ten dollars and he accepted it—he even threw in this case."

Suitably impressed, we all said, "That is a miracle!" and applauded his good fortune.

"No," he said, his green eyes twinkling, "that's not the miracle." He went into another long story describing the community he lived with, a small tent city under an overpass. And how after his good fortune scoring the flute, he took it back to his tent and put it inside. A night of drinking and partying with his homeless companions led to a blackout. When he awoke the next day, the beautiful instrument was gone.

His heart was sick—he had been so elated with his blessing and now he was as depressed as he had been joyful. He said he was too sad to yell or carry on; he simply sat and cried. Soon someone from the community noticed and asked why he was crying, and the story of the stolen flute spread through the camp like wildfire. No one claimed to know anything, and they all set about searching for it. "Maybe you were so drunk you don't remember what you did with it?"

"No!" he exclaimed. "I was not so drunk I would lose the flute I love. I lost it once—I would not have lost it again." All day they searched while, our new friend said, he sat and wept.

When he woke the next morning, the flute in its beat-up black case was sitting by his head, as if it had never been taken! Again, we were amazed, and again we all exclaimed, "Now that is a miracle!"

And again he said, "That is not the miracle I wanted to share with you."

Now his eyes were like emeralds, dancing with energy. He carefully took out each piece of the flute, caressing them with his fingers of bronze like a lover, or a soft newborn baby. He fitted each piece together and tested the keys. Then he closed his bright eyes and began to play.

The music lifted up through the green of the trees on the parkway, up through the fluffy summer clouds, up past the punishing sun, up to heaven. Within a few minutes, I was wiping tears off my face, and as I looked at Marge, Donna, and my other friends, I saw they too were crying.

The song he was playing was "Amazing Grace," and never have I heard it played so beautifully. He wove together two or three hymns I was familiar with, always coming back to the refrain that we all sang silently in our heads as he played the notes. "Amazing grace, how sweet the sound, that saved a wretch like me. I once was lost but now I'm found, was blind but now I see."

We stood in stunned silence when he finished the song. Silently he bowed his head, and then he prayed for us. For my unborn daughter, for each of us to be happy and content in life. When I opened my eyes, I met his, and with a twinkle and a radiant smile, he said, "*That's the miracle.*"

You've read my stories by now and know that I grew up in a small-town bubble. It wasn't until I grew up and out of that environment that I was exposed to a big, wide world of diversity. The melting pot of life. Differences of color, culture, talent, and opinion.

In our present world, we are exposed to a lot more diversity online, through social media—people post their feelings and political agendas, and information is overflowing to us. It's a world of abundant information, like-minded and differing views right at our fingertips. It's amazing to have endless knowledge available to us and to be so connected to so many people at the click of a mouse or just by looking down at our phone. But is it the answer to learning about and loving on people? I doubt it.

Who could've known the homeless man on the street would give me such a gift that day? This person I was so far from being able to understand, whose shoes I could not fill, whose story I couldn't relate to, whose skin or gender I couldn't identify with, whose talent I couldn't match—this man blessed my life and touched my soul with his music and his faith. It was one of those unexpected moments in time when God showed up as an angel in disguise. In that moment, I wasn't concerned with his appearance, nor did I care about the foolish choices he made in his life; I was mesmerized by the grace-filled sound coming out of his flute. In that moment, I appreciated he was willing to step out of his comfort zone to approach us and share his miracle with us. I gave him a sandwich; in return he gave me everything he had. That kind of exchange doesn't happen online.

My daughter Blessing quite literally *forged* her way ahead in bringing another foreign exchange student into our home and our life. This young girl who had nothing, who went from neglect, abuse, and malnourishment to having the extreme opposite in a house full of siblings and family, wanted to open her home again to yet another person. Similar to my street friend in Philly, she wanted to share what she had and cherished the most with another person. And again, when I accepted her plea and went along with her forgery, boy, was I blessed! To see my children prepare for Toni's arrival and accept him into our home with welcoming arms. To learn about Toni's culture and lifestyle, and watch him step out of *his* comfort zone and grow into a farm boy!

Generally speaking, we seek out people who are like-minded, who think like us, who hold the same values, maybe worship the same way. We meet a lot of people, but we *befriend* people we make natural connections with, and that's just human nature. Here's the thing, though—there will be times in our lives when an unnatural connection will be made. We'll make the acquaintance with someone who is so far different from us that nothing about it makes sense—except that maybe we're supposed to step outside our comfort zone and talk for a bit. See the differences and appreciate them. At the very least, respect them.

CHAPTER 11:
A CONNECTED HEART

Mom was big—that's the only way I can describe her. She had a wide-open face with sparkling green eyes. Wilma Dean had a big smile and an even bigger laugh. She was six feet tall, and she had big bones. She wasn't fat, she was just, well, *big*. She filled a room with her presence. In the fifties she would have been called a dame or maybe a broad. Today women get offended by these terms, but I smile when I hear them, thinking of Mom.

She usually had a cigarette lit and a cup of black coffee close by. She wasn't radical about anything, and she didn't conform to anyone's expectations. Dad tried to control her, down to the clothes she was allowed to wear, but somehow that still didn't confine or constrict her big personality. Mom was a teen in the fifties, and while many of her contemporaries were putting flowers in their hair and getting high the following decade, Mom was home with kids pulling on her skirt as she planted veggies in the garden and splatter painting her kitchen floor pink and brown, since there was no money to buy linoleum.

When she was young, Mom wore red lipstick and pedal pushers and looked like a movie star. As she got older, she still wore red lipstick, and she thought that was enough, even with curlers in her hair. She would tie a bandana over the wire rollers, put her red lipstick on, light a cigarette, and head for school to pick us up out of the rain. I would die a thousand deaths of embarrassment that she was in public with curlers in her hair and try to walk the other direction. "Get in the damn car, Rene, you are getting soaked to the bone," she would say. *Damn* was her favorite word. The damn car. The damn rabbit that bit DeAnna. The damn rain. The damn teacher that gave too damned much homework. It's a good word and fits for any occasion. "I don't give a damn what time you think you have to be at school, you are going to sit down and eat breakfast," or "Dammit, Rene, get in here and finish these dishes."

Along with her big bones and her big feet, I also inherited the damn gene. In the same tone with the same inflections, I have become her voice of damnation! Today I stubbed my toe and screamed, "Dammit!" and then I laughed at how I open my mouth and my mother comes out.

Mom was an early bird; Dad was a night owl. Mom was always up before anyone else in the house, and until I was in high school and just coming home at the break of dawn after sneaking out all night, she was the first one to pad around the floor in her big, bare feet and had the coffee brewing before anyone else was ready to stir. On more than one occasion, I jumped in the shower after climbing in the back window, pretending that I had been up and running for exercise when really I had been out all night with Dee Dee or my boyfriend, racing down to the beach or sneaking into the high school to play a prank.

Wilma Dean was spontaneous. She would wake us up on a Saturday morning and say, "Get your coats on, we're going for a ride." The four of us kids and our neighbor Dallen would pile into the family station wagon and take off on one of her adventures. Most often we would go to the beach after a storm to search for the round glass Japanese fishing floats and beautiful pieces of driftwood. Sometimes we went during a storm to watch the mountainous waves crash over the jetty in a deafening roar and witness the power of lightning striking on the horizon above the blackened sky of the Pacific Ocean.

Mom would take us berry picking in the forests and fields near our home in the spring, or up to the coastal mountains to hunt for mushrooms or huckleberries. Sometimes we would sneak onto old farms or find an abandoned orchard and pick apples that fell to the ground. Mom insisted if they weren't being used and had just been left to rot, then we weren't stealing them. To this day I adhere to that philosophy and have taken my kids picking fruit in abandoned orchards on a number of occasions...

okay, I admit sometimes the orchards weren't that abandoned... okay, I will pick apples off the ground of someone's property in the middle of a crowded suburb if I see they're going to waste. Our little town now offers a map for gleaners of abandoned fruit trees so people can salvage the food before it goes to waste. Mom would like that.

Mom didn't really care what other people thought. I loved that about her. If there is one quality or trait I hope to keep alive in her memory, it is that one. She would wear what she wanted, eat what she wanted (pickled pigs' feet and okra come to mind), say what she felt, and didn't conform to anyone's standards—except for Dad's. Whether she was afraid of his temper or wanted to please him, I don't know, but he was the only person whose opinion seemed to carry any weight with Mom. She didn't care that she wasn't a part of the country club set or that she wasn't invited to play bridge with the popular women in our little town. She didn't ever try to impress anyone or pretend to be someone she was not. By the time I was old enough to be aware of such things, I loved that Mom was comfortable in her own skin. I remember her telling me stories of how shy and embarrassed she had been as a child, ashamed of her tall stature, ashamed of her Arkansas drawl when she moved to Oregon as a teen, and embarrassed by her size-twelve feet and the fact that no nice shoes ever fit. But by the time she had given birth to the four of us kids, she was completely at home in her height, her big feet, her silly southern sayings, and her own personality.

Mom wasn't a good student and had no formal education past high school. Neither did either of her

parents, and no one in our immediate family really val-
ued or encouraged academia. But Wilma Dean was a
lifelong learner. She was naturally curious about her sur-
roundings and the natural world. Next to her passion
and zeal for having adventures, she was passionate about
learning. She would investigate every creepy, crawly, fur-
ry creature she encountered with the encyclopedia set in
our hallway, or at the library, and figure out what exactly
the living thing was. She loved to learn of our native
flora and fauna; she studied trees and bees and edible,
medicinal, and house plants. She loved antiquity, archi-
tecture, all things made of wood and anything shiny.
She instilled in all four of her children a passion to learn
about the world we live in.

When a cloud would pass overhead, she would study
it and ask, "Now, why is that cloud so fluffy when the
other clouds are so flat?" or "Now, why do you think
the water is so much darker today than when we were
here at the ocean yesterday?" And then she would try to
figure it out.

"Now, why is that?" was a favorite Wilma expression, next to "dammit." If I complained about something
or talked about a social injustice or something I felt was
wrong, she would tilt her head to the side, take a drag off
her cigarette, and look me in the eye and say, "Now, why is
that?" A rhetorical comment that was more of a challenge
than a question. Her three living children ask that question constantly. Now why is it that grocery stores throw
away perfectly good food while kids go to bed hungry?

Mom had books about statues of Chinese warriors;
books about Tutankhamen, the child pharaoh; books

on healing herbs and women's medical issues; books on everything from how marbles were made to antelopes and aardvarks. And she stored the most amazing pieces of worthless information in her head only to randomly declare over dinner, "Did you know that King Tut was probably an ugly child with funny legs?" or "I hear the smelt are running tonight—do you kids want to go smelt dipping after the dishes are done?"

Smelt dipping. Crabbing off the docks. Berry picking. Apple stealing. Sledding in the snow at midnight. Skinny-dipping under the falls. Sliding down a sand dune on a board, or racing across the dunes in a buggy. Deer hunting. Snipe hunting. Treasure hunting. Bargain hunting. Dancing all night long with red lipstick, ratted hair, Aqua Net, and bell-bottom pantsuits. Mom slept little, lived off burned toast, cigarettes, and black coffee, and taught us how to live life fully. She died at fifty-seven but lived more in those years than many who live to be a hundred.

The smell of roses, honeysuckle, wild mint, and salt air all transport me to my paternal grandparents' house by the bay. The hours we spent digging clams, finding tiny crabs hiding beneath barnacle-encrusted rocks, collecting seashells, and building sand castles are engrained in my memory like etchings on granite. I can't remember important things, like what time a wedding is set to start or where I parked my car, but ridiculous details that mean nothing, mean everything.

I remember the scents of life most of all. The heady scent of lilacs in bloom take me back to my parents' rented farmhouse up Lillian Slough, and picking them to make a bouquet for my mom. I smell hay as it's being cut so it can dry in the sun, and I'm a farm girl again watching my older brother, Matt, throw the heavy bales up on the wagon to get stored in the barn for winter.

From these memories and images, I've tried to fashion a life for my children. If given the choice between a fabulous trip for myself and my husband to a four-star hotel on a sunny beach in the Caribbean or a week at our shore cottage on the chilly coast of Washington State with a dozen kids and a few wet dogs tracking in sand, I take the kids hands down. For me there's no pleasure in luxury unless it is shared with as many as possible.

I try to overshadow the bad memories, the fights I witnessed with my parents and grandparents, the cruelty of men in my family to the women that loved them, and I hold fast to the small details, aromas, sounds and songs that brought me joy. Then I try to recreate those memories, and I infuse them with as much love as I can muster and give them to my children and the multitude of other kids I have been blessed to love.

I loved sitting around the bonfire when we went camping, listening to my dad and our friends play the guitar and sing silly songs deep into the starry night. I love the smell of campfire smoke in my hair, because that is the smell of family time. On my farm, we have three or four fire pits for campfires. We have one on the patio in the backyard right off the kitchen. It's a rock fireplace that I designed for one reason: because I wanted one like my grandparents had, made of native stone in their backyard.

Delilah

The best memories I have of my grandparents come from sitting around that fire, roasting hot dogs and marshmallows and listening to my grandpa tell ridiculous stories. He was missing both of his little fingers and told us kids one was lost from picking his nose and the other got run over by a steamboat...

So I tell my kids silly stories and we play guessing games around the campfire. Shaylah is a young adult now, but when she was in high school, it wasn't unusual for her to say to me while I was getting ready to wrap up the night and close up the house, "Mom, is it okay if a few friends come over for a bonfire?"

"Define few," I'd reply, already knowing the answer.

Within minutes (because, well, social media) the cars would come down the long gravel drive, the dogs would start barking, and within half an hour her entire high school choir would be assembled around the campfire up on the hill. Sometimes I'd join them to deliver sodas and s'more fixings, sometimes I'd climb the stairs to our prayer tower and open the windows and listen. It didn't usually take long before they would break into song and start harmonizing around the roaring fire. I have tucked those memories in my heart right next to the ones of my dad singing around the campfire when I was a kid growing up in Oregon.

Shay has graduated from high school now and moved on with her life. Her younger brothers and sisters are the ones having bonfires beneath the canopy of evergreens, and their group of friends don't spontaneously break into Broadway tunes or seventeenth-century carols as Shay's did, but their conversations are just as enlightening and their time under the stars just as enriching for them.

It's not difficult to create opportunities for memories, but it requires being 100 percent present. You have to turn off the TV, get off the damn computer, and be fully focused on the present in order to have the experiences that will be woven into the tapestry of your family history.

Sadly, most of us are too busy or too distracted to see the opportunities to create memories. It's easy to get caught up in being successful, working out, being active in clubs and organizations, going to church, etc.—not that these things are bad, but often they become so time-consuming and our schedules so full, there is little room for spontaneity and creativity. By being too focused or busy, you miss the opportunities to just be silly, excited, daring, and fun!

I have a dear friend who was once a workaholic, and it was killing him when we first met. Okay, maybe not killing him, but certainly taking a toll on his family. His kids saw him on weekends, and even then he was often working on his computer or taking business calls. We were to take a business trip one time and I insisted we drive. Why, he wanted to know, when we could get there in half an hour if we flew. It would take hours to drive.

I tried to explain the beauty of the terrain we would be going through, mountains and valleys and huge forests that are hundreds of years of old-growth timber. "We can get out and hike! The rocks and trails are breathtaking, and I'll show you a swimming hole my mom once took me to so us girls could go skinny-dipping." His reply has become a running joke between us: "Anything I need to see, I can see from the front window."

The truth is anything and everything you *need* to see can't be seen from a car window, or from a picturesque photograph someone posted on social media, for that matter. Old-growth timber that reaches to the heavens, wildflowers in a field, kids singing around a campfire, swimming holes in placid rivers, crawdads in shallow streams, city lights at night, the buzz of people watching and tossing Frisbees on a sunny day in a city park, a plush little couch in a corner coffee shop hosting an intimate conversation... These things can't be seen from a car. They need to be experienced with all your senses. And when you smell them, touch them, hear them, feel the moment, drink in their majesty, the memories will be etched on your heart as in granite.

Digital media is both a blessing and a curse. I believe we need to stay vigilant. A babysitter who allowed our children to witness violence or played games that involved stealing cars, shooting people, or destroying communities would never be tolerated, but many kids spend hours and hours with these babysitters we call computer games. I'm sure you've heard of couples who have hit dead ends in their relationships and marriages that have suffered and failed because social media became their partner's lover. Instead of romantic nights snuggling and talking in bed, the TV flickers blue light into the darkness and all conversation is lost in favor of canned laugh tracks and late-night talk show hosts.

I can't tell you how many hundreds of women have called my show over the years, feeling completely abandoned and alone because their husbands came home from work, sat in front of the TV for hours, stumbled off to bed after falling asleep in the easy chair, and never connected with them on an emotional level. Statistics show that young children spend about as much time watching TV and playing on electronic devices as they spend in school. When do they have time to ride their bikes? Play hide-and-seek? Read books? Climb trees? Pull pranks? Build forts? Do chores? Learn to live life? Stay vigilant. Please.

When my grandfather was a young boy, school lasted through eighth grade, and then children were expected work on their family farm. Grandpa Mac (McGowne) knew how to do a man's work by the time he was twelve, how to drive a team of horses, saddle them, and take care of their hooves. He could chop wood, build a fire, cook for a family, and do the dishes. He knew how to survive in a difficult world, and he and my grandma passed that wisdom on to my mother, who in turn passed it on to her four kids. I've tried to pass what I know on to my children, but it is so difficult in today's world where working with your hands and your wits seems more a lifestyle choice than a necessity.

We live in a world that glamorizes greed and sloth, where the Kardashians are admired and emulated because of physical beauty and material possessions. In order to change the world, you have to be able to navigate the world, contribute to the world, get involved with your world, and you can't do that when you are numb to reality because you are engaged in hours and hours of media each day. Stay vigilant.

When I started working in Ghana, in 2004, one of the first things that shocked me was seeing young children, only eight or nine years old, running out into busy inter-sections, selling things from cartons held on top of their heads. In the villages where I work and visit, I see toddlers helping their moms, sweeping the hard-packed dirt with a broom fashioned from twigs tied tightly together. My daughter Blessing was almost three years old when I met her. Her tiny body was tight like steel, and her little arms and legs were muscled like an athlete's. She was used to walking for miles, carrying a bucket of water on her head. In Africa, children are taught from birth that they are a part of a family, part of a village, part of a tribe, and they are expected to contribute and help—like in my grand-parents' day, survival depends upon it.

Here in the US, children are crippled by adults doing everything for them. Kids who help with chores in the home often get a reward or an allowance, instead of being taught that is their contribution to the well-being of their family. Not that we shouldn't teach our kids the value of money and help them to work to earn some on their own, but I believe simple chores like washing the dishes or vac-uuming the floor should be a part of their daily routine; it's what comes from being a part of something bigger than oneself.

Kids are crippled emotionally when they are protected from negative experiences and personal challenges, from the bumps and bruises of life, by claiming unfairness for a lower grade than expected or less playing time than want-ed on a team, by parents stepping in when an altercation arises between peers. Under these well-intentioned paren-tal assists, they don't have the ability to learn personal ac-countability and responsibility in a way that allows them to bravely navigate the world and think of others' needs and feelings as well as their own.

Our modern world poses a real conundrum to parents raising children. In a world of overabundance, overmechanization, overexposure to media, how does one raise ambitious, self-sufficient, caring, compassionate kids?

I strongly believe we are hurting our kids by not allowing them to get dirty, not allowing them to climb trees and ride bikes. We all need to be exposed to nature; even if you live in a jumbled jungle of a city, you need to find opportunities to walk under the broad expanse of an open sky, watch squirrels looking for nuts in a city park, feed pigeons as they land close enough to touch.

I see a lot of ads on billboards, the Internet, and in magazines touting the latest drug, device, or insurance program for our health needs. It's simply a bandage over a bigger problem. Going outside, walking in the rain, planting flowers and edibles, eating the vegetables and fresh fruit, *that* is health care. I want my kids to get dirty, to roll in the mud and play in the streams. I want them to slip and stumble and to get scraped knees, because I want them to experience the beauty God has created all around us. A person can't get engaged in saving natural resources, in fighting for the lives of sea mammals and endangered species, in worrying about the changing climate of our planet or the pollution in our drinking water if they have no connection to the natural world except through TV programming.

I got a call from Sonny (now going by Isaiah) one day as he was on his way home from a fourteen-hour shift as a police officer. When I asked him if he was going home to sleep, he said, "No, I'm making breakfast for the kids and taking them to church and then on a bear hunt." We both laughed; he doesn't really hunt bear, nor would he take his four kids—all under the age of nine—on a bear hunt. But when he was a toddler, we lived next to a big park in West Seattle and I would take him on long hikes through the majestic Douglas fir and madrone, the huckleberry bushes and salal, and along our trek we would "hunt" for bear. I taught him to search high and low for signs of tracks, scat, and spots beneath bushes or trees where they might curl up in slumber. There were no bear in the park and I knew that, but at four years old, he was excited to search for wildlife, to watch the squirrels running and playing, the crows flying overhead. We'd stuff our pockets with bird-seed and sprinkle it along the trail for the wild birds to enjoy, and on more than one occasion we put marshmallows on tree limbs and left them for the "bear" to discover. Today he and his family live in a beautiful community next to a green space, and his kids excitedly go on long hikes, searching for the bear they might discover living in the woods.

Wilma Dean had it right. Wake the kids on a Saturday morning and surprise them with an adventure to somewhere that isn't a virtual reality. It's hard to replicate those days of old before the Internet and technology came blazing through and took over our social agendas. There is a big place for the Internet and social media and virtual connections—I love connecting with my friends and family and fans on Facebook, I do. But I love, love, *love* the moments off-line when I'm making real inter-personal connections, when my kids are having real-life conversations around a fire pit, when memories are being made, and the scent of a moment is being registered in my brain, when a moment in time is encapsulated by a song forever. In a world where we've become desensitized with too much information, it's so important to get off-line and make real connections with people in order to feel again. The information will always be out there in cyberspace when we need it, but genuine feelings can only occur in real life.

If we are going to change the world, one heart at a time, we must make sure we and those closest to us are fully engaged and aware of the beauty of the natural world, fully engaged in real life, real connections, real human and nature interactive experiences. We should be more excited about reality than reality shows. Trust me, I've been on enough TV production sets that I can assure you there is nothing real about reality shows.

What if you took it upon yourself to spend time with a young person, instilling in them something to care about? Horseback riding, swimming, drawing, skateboarding, foreign language, singing, cycling, hiking, reading, carpentry, welding, knitting, cooking, chess, card games? What is your hobby and how did you come to it? Have you passed it down to the next generation? Have you been open-minded about letting your child try a new hobby or skill, even if it's not something that suits you? Believe in a young person, and you will change the world for that person. Teach a young person that talking

Delilah

is better than texting and that *reality* is better than *virtual reality*—and indeed you will be doing that child and this world a great service.

CHAPTER 12:
A HEART THAT ENDURES

I was twenty-four when I had my firstborn son, Isaiah. His father nicknamed him Sonny when he was just a few days old, and that name stuck until he was grown and out of the house. George and I divorced when Sonny was a baby, and when he was two, his dad moved to San Francisco. He didn't see his father except for a handful of times until he was in high school. His dad was a news reporter, a rabid sports fan, and an alcoholic, not necessarily in that order.

There's an old song by Bobby Hebb called "Sunny." I don't think that was the motivation behind George choosing that nickname, but the lyrics certainly are apropos: *"Sunny, thank you for the truth you let me see... and Sunny, thank you for your love from A to Z... Now the dark days are gone, and the bright days are here, my Sunny one shines so sincere. Sunny one so true, I love you..."*

Sonny went from being a chubby baby boy to a long, lean child with a natural curiosity for all God's handiwork. He was fascinated by the simple things in life; he loved to camp, to listen to me tell stories in a darkened tent, and to eat scrambled eggs cooked over an open fire. He could have cared less if he wore the same pair of sweatpants ten days in a row, and I often marvel that he was the only child I ever had who slept in on Christmas morning. He didn't care about the presents under the tree and rarely asked for a specific gift. In fact, until he was probably seven or eight, he was far more interested in the boxes than the gifts that came in them... so I would get big packing boxes from Sears and construct forts and sailing ships and trains out of them. Sonny loved life, and he loved the people closest to him. He was, and is, a homebody. Such a homebody in fact that for a few years, while he and his wife, Riely, were getting established in the world, they lived with their four children in the last home he lived in as a teen. My grandchildren were able to enjoy the fire pit I made years ago for Sonny and his friends to roast marshmallows around. What joy it gave me to see his young family sitting around the fire singing the silly songs I sang to him as a young boy.

Even after giving birth to another daughter and adopting three siblings, I was convinced, mostly due to Sonny's

Jesus-like goodness (I'm not making that up, he was given the Most Jesus-Like award in school), that I was a terrific mom. Then came Zack.

The loud, squirming kids I once smugly observed while pushing Sonny in the cart? The kids destroying the neatly stacked displays of shiny apples? Now I was the mom trying to pick the tumbling fruit up off the floor as Zack gleefully reached for the bottom apple on the pyramid. Zack was as fearless and high-strung as Sonny was cautious and quiet.

Zack was a live wire from day one. He was generally unsettled, needed me more, followed directions less, and lived for *action*! Stubborn, fearless, and saw rules as lines to be crossed. In truth, he's a lot more like me in many ways than his older brother...

But he was more than just a bundle of energy and a headstrong kid. Zack often wouldn't eat and became frighteningly thin as a toddler. He was rarely content, didn't bond with people well, and wasn't meeting the expected benchmarks for development. At two, we had him evaluated and were told that he was definitely on the autistic spectrum. Thankfully, there was an early-intervention program available that allowed Zack to receive occupational and other helpful therapies. We were counseled on how to distract and redirect, how to choose our battles... We celebrated his obsession with the color green with painted bedroom walls, green pants, green shirts, green toys.

He was a study in contrasts. A boy with big eyes and an enormous and tender heart, who perceived life on an uncommonly high level, which caused him both physical and emotional pain. Zack would often come up with in-genious plans that often backfired and that, after the ini-tial panic and commotion was over, gave us stories that you just can't make up. Like this:

One spring day when Zack was twelve, I yelled out-side for him to come to dinner. When he didn't respond, I asked the other kids where he was, and they replied they thought he was up in the neighborhood with his buddies. When we couldn't find him after about half an hour, I started to get nervous, calling his name louder and louder. Coming back into the house, I yelled his name at the top of my lungs, and a groggy Zack rose from the couch and asked what I wanted.

I hadn't even seen him there. Zack rarely slows down enough to take a nap, and in fact, I'd never even seen him sleep on the living room couch before. I chastised him for not letting me know where he was and told him to wash up and get ready for dinner. Quietly he told me he wasn't feeling well, that he had no appetite and he was going to go upstairs and go to bed. I started to snap at him that he still needed to eat something when I looked at his face and noticed he was white as a sheet.

When I asked him what was wrong, he took off his baseball cap and pulled his long bangs off his forehead; he had a bump larger than a goose egg, and his entire forehead was red. I asked him what happened and he said, "It's kind of a long story, but I really don't feel good."

I threw him in the car and raced to the urgent care about ten minutes away. When I went to check in, they told us to have a seat and they would see him as soon as they could. I frantically said, "I think he's got a traumatic head injury—can you please see him now?"

The woman at the front desk was trying her best to calm me when Zack bent over and began throwing up blood. She yelled for a nurse to come out, and they got him into a room. The doctor who was on call that day told me to calm down and said that they needed to get him to a hospital immediately. Zack was loaded in the back of an ambulance and I was allowed to ride with him as we were rushed to Mary Bridge Children's Hospital. As soon as we got there, the doctor explained that he probably didn't have any broken bones, but that he did have a large contusion and they were going to do some imaging.

While we waited for them to get him in to do an MRI, the story began to unfold... He'd gone up to the neighborhood to play with the kids a few weeks prior and found a dead squirrel. Zack and his friends thought that it would be best if they buried said squirrel. After a week or two passed, they decided to go find out if the squirrel had decomposed into a skeleton or remained intact.

Much to their delight when they dug up the unfortunate critter, the boys discovered it was partially decomposed, but even better, filled with maggots. (If you find their delight in this disgusting discovery strange, you haven't spent much time around adolescent boys!)

Once the poor, maggot-infested squirrel was retrieved from its peaceful grave in the ground, they decided to be creative and use it to torment one of the girls in the neighborhood.

The boys found a strong young sapling that they decided to use as a catapult (or in this case a squirrel-a-pult). They took the top of the tree (which was about nine feet tall) and pulled it down to the ground. One boy sat on the ground holding tight to the top while the other one used a stick to lay the carcass across the branches of the tree. When they were ready, the boy seated released the tree, causing the squirrel to launch through the air and into the yard of an unsuspecting neighbor girl. Their first attempt failed miserably, and instead the squirrel was flung hard against the ground just a few feet in front of them. Using all their mathematical genius, they recalculated and recalibrated and figured out if they moved the squirrel closer to the top of the tree, the projection would be farther.

This time Zack gingerly placed the rotting squirrel on the uppermost branches. The boy holding the tree thought Zack was finished and released his hold, however, Zack had not yet moved out of the way.

The tree smacked my son right above the bridge of his nose in the middle of his forehead. He was knocked backward, and he thinks he might've even blacked out for a moment before he managed to stumble home and find his way to the couch.

After hearing his account of things, I didn't know if I should laugh or cry, and I think I did both. But my laughter was quickly squelched when the doctor walked in the room and asked to see me in the hallway. He pulled out images and said, "Your son's skull is fractured in at least eight places where the tree struck him." Now I was scared.

The doctor looked at me and asked how the incident happened. I said, "You're never going to believe this... But please tell me what the dangers are now."

He said there was great danger of the brain swelling, that Zack's forehead might be disfigured and that he might require surgery. For the next ten to twelve hours, they were going to keep him under observation and watch for symptoms of brain bleeding or swelling, as well as closely monitor his vital signs and mental alertness. After that, they would figure out what the next step should be. He said he was going to have Zack assessed by a plastic surgeon to see what kind of surgery might be necessary to repair any disfiguration that might occur.

When I walked back in the room and told Zack the news, he broke into a broad smile, and asked, "Do I get to count this as eight broken bones or just one?"

He liked to keep track of his broken bones, because at age twelve he had already had at least seven. He considered each one a badge of honor.

I spent the night in an uncomfortable chair next to my son's hospital bed, praying that he wouldn't have brain damage or any long-term issues. I thought about his handsome face and any surgery he might require. I thought about what might have happened if he had remained asleep on the couch and I hadn't screamed to wake him...

The next day another doctor took more images and came into the room in shock. Each little piece of bone that had been broken and pushed inward had moved back into perfect placement. There didn't appear to be any swelling to the brain, and the surgeon they had requested was on standby but wouldn't be coming in to see me.

Instead, an expert in traumatic head injuries came to visit and talk with me. "No jumping, no running, no video games for two weeks, and plenty of rest," she said, handed me her card, and left. Children's Hospital kept him one more night for observations and sent him home.

God healed him completely with no necessary medical intervention. A few years later Zack didn't even have a scar from the experience, but our family would groan each time we saw roadkill, and we'd always ask Zacky if he wanted to try to use it on a catapult...

My Zacky loved music and memorized lyrics like I do, but let's just say his favorite genres were a wee bit different than adult contemporary. Zack excelled at some subjects, but the linear timeline of school, homework, and testing never worked for him well, so school was a struggle. That said, he was still super bright and extremely witty.

Life with Zack was a magical mystery tour, to be sure, but I think God gave me my Zack Attack to teach me to love deeper, practice patience, and to know I'd never have the final say in things.

Our lives are like that—Zack story after Zack story. The stuff of great legend and side-splitting hilarity. His one little heart was involved in some very big miracles.

I am not the only one who grieves and has trouble coping with the day to day. Zachariah and Shaylah are the two biological children I share with their father, Doug Ortega. Shaylah learned the day after her twenty-third birthday, the day before her little brother took his life, that she was pregnant. Her world, as mine, will never be the same. Her siblings, her dad, grandparents, aunts, uncles, cousins; the waves of grief wash over us all in ever-widening circles. Shaylah, my baby now having a baby, and her heart in shreds...

For as strong and unbreakable and healthy that Sonny was, Shaylah was quite the opposite. From birth Sonny was fat and healthy. He never broke a bone or caught a cold. He didn't get sick when he was teething or when cold and flu season came around. He didn't fuss or cry when it was time to take a nap and he loved to sleep, curled up in my arms, all night long.

His little sister, Shaylah, ten years younger, was a chubby, sweet newborn, but when she was just a few weeks old, she started throwing up when she would nurse. She got a fever and runny nose when her teeth started coming in. Her left eye was weak, and when she was tired it would cross slightly. She was treated for the flu or a cold every other week, it seemed.

My life was in complete turmoil during my pregnancy with Shay and in the first few years of her young life. The radio station I was on in Philly, WMGK, fired me when I was seven months pregnant. Getting fired was nothing new, getting fired when I was pregnant was... We had to pack up our life and move back to Boston right after Shay was born. Lucky for me I had held onto the house I owned there.

When WMGK fired me, I thought my world was going to implode. But God was there to see me through. The station manager, Tyler, arranged to let me go prior to my contract being up. And they agreed to pay me a large bonus I had earned, based on my ratings, at the end of my contract, which meant I would still be on payroll through Shaylah's birth and into the holidays. What a blessing I didn't have to worry about my pregnancy and delivery being covered by insurance!

When Shay was two, she had a cold that turned into a fever and she couldn't breathe, so I called 911 and an ambulance took her to Swedish Hospital in Seattle. They diagnosed her with respiratory syncytial virus and after two days sent us home. Two months later, while I was in downtown Seattle in my studio on the air, my friend Jill was babysitting her and Sonny. Jill called my hotline and said, "You need to come home, Shaylah is running a high fever." I taped out my show, got in the car, and raced home. When I got there, Shay was indeed running a fever, and she was coughing constantly. I ran a tepid bath and got in with her, holding her burning little body to mine, and then I started to run cold water to cool her down. She coughed and then stopped breathing. I screamed to Jill to call 911 as I tried to revive her, trying to remember the CPR instructions I had learned years before in my Red Cross training course. Shaylah's lips turned blue, and her eyes rolled back into her head.

It only took the fire truck about three minutes to reach my house—the fire station was a few blocks away. The firemen and paramedics that arrived took her from me and continued to perform CPR, strapped her to a small gurney and got her into the ambulance. I threw on some jeans and a sweatshirt and rode in the back with her. I had never prayed so hard in all my life as I did in that ambulance. It raced screaming through the night to Seattle

Children's Hospital. When we arrived they rushed her into the ER and made me stay behind while they worked to save her life. Her heart stopped at one point, and they had to restart it. They finally stabilized her, and she was intubated to force air in and out of her lungs.

When the crisis had subsided, the doctor who saved Shaylah came to speak to me and explain what had happened. Her first question to me was, "How long has your daughter suffered with asthma?"

Asthma? "She doesn't have asthma," I said. "She had RSV a few times, but I don't know what you mean by asthma."

"Your daughter was in a full-blown asthma attack. Her airways were completely shut down. Her oxygen levels were in the sixties before we got her intubated. She technically died once, but we were able to get her heart restarted. How long has your daughter had asthma?"

I stood in stunned silence, trying to grasp what this young doctor was saying. My daughter had something called asthma. She had technically died. She was on a machine to keep her alive. And I had no clue what asthma was outside of being told my firstborn sometimes had a hard time breathing when he ran too hard in sports, and one doctor had suggested he had exercise-induced asthma.

The next day I was asked to attend a class that Children's Hospital put on for parents of asthmatic children. There were two other parents in the class, and all three of us sat in numbed silence for the first half hour, trying to grasp what was going on in our children's bodies.

The fevers, the hundreds of times Shay would start coughing in the middle of the night, the multiple trips to urgent care, and the last trip to the ER. The many diagnoses of flu, colds, RSV. The struggle to keep weight on her after she learned to crawl and the blue tint her hands and lips would often get... and now I was told my daughter had pneumonia, that her right lung was almost half filled with fluid and that she had reactive airways and severe asthma.

Although she was stable, it took two days to wean her off the ventilator and begin our new normal of life with a medically fragile child.

I couldn't let Shaylah cry, because crying would cause her throat to close down and her windpipe to swell, and after a few minutes of crying she would be choking for air, unable to breathe. As a result I would jump through hoops to keep her from coughing, crying, or getting emotionally distraught. She was tested for allergies in a macabre exam that involved a grid being drawn on her back, followed by between fifty and one hundred pinpricks. To help her endure this torture I took off my shirt and held her to my chest as the nurse pricked her tender flesh over and over and over. After her skin was assaulted, the nurse swabbed on a multitude of common allergens—tree nuts, ground nuts, wheat, egg, grass, pollen—and then they observed the grid for a reaction. Within minutes her soft white flesh was red, swollen, and angry. The results? She was basically allergic to life. Mold, dust, certain plastics, cleaning fluids, all nuts, soy, dust mites, cats, dogs, bird feathers... the list was immense.

Nut allergies were the most dangerous, followed closely by mold and dust mites. The hospital offered a class for parents of allergy-prone/asthmatic kids. Thank God! It was Breathing 101 for me.

I went home and ripped out all the carpet in our tiny house. Then I went down to the basement and evaluated the mold situation. I had owned the house for seventeen years at that point, and it was a little old shack when I bought it. I knew there was little I could do about the moldy basement, nor could I remove the neighbor's trees that towered overhead and spread thick pollen in the spring.

A few weeks later I found a house on the same street, just seven doors down, that had a dry basement, a treeless yard, and hardwood floors. It was not as old as the tiny cottage I had purchased at twenty-one, and was more than twice the size of my thousand-square-foot home.

I bought the house, and we packed up and moved down the street. I dug up the plants that I had just planted the year before, many that I had moved to Seattle from Boston.

With hardwood floors, a dry and mold-free basement, no trees in the yard, and daily medications, Shaylah's health began to improve. Day by day her pale skin got a bit rosier and the nighttime asthma attacks got a little more manageable. Oh, but how my life had changed.

When Sonny was young and we were alone, I thought nothing of throwing a cast-iron skillet, an ice chest full of food, a large sleeping bag, and a tent in the back of my beat-up car and taking off for the mountains. We camped along creeks and streams, hiked the Olympic trail and slept under the stars if it was warm enough. We camped along the Washington and Oregon coast, and when we moved to Boston we camped nearly every weekend in the summer months. I bought a dirt bike and better hiking boots for Sonny, so we could explore the deciduous forests of Maine and Massachusetts, the White Mountains and Cape Cod. After I married Doug, he joined us on some of our camping excursions, but he never seemed to enjoy the outdoors as much as Sonny and I did. I even took Sonny and a neighbor camping when I was eight months pregnant with Shaylah.

Looking back I wonder how Sonny didn't lose his mind when I married Doug. He had gone from being an only child who had no real rules and my 100 percent focus and adoration to living with a stepdad who didn't quite understand our way of life and having a baby sister who was always sick.

Now that Shaylah had been diagnosed with asthma and allergies, it was almost as if we had to keep her in a bubble. She was allergic to changes in the weather! If the temperature varied more than ten to twenty degrees, if she went from a warm house to a freezing, snowy day, even if she were bundled up in a snowsuit and hat, her face would be covered with hives and her airways would shut down. Same if she was outside on a hot day and jumped or fell into a cold stream—her lungs would cease to work and her bronchial tubes would swell and close down.

She was so allergic to nuts, just sitting next to someone on a plane who opened a package of peanuts would cause her to vomit and start coughing. She was allergic to pollen from flowers and trees and grasses, so hiking in the woods was out of the question, as was swimming in a mountain stream. The few times I tried to take her to a ski lodge, it took twenty-four-hour vigilance just to keep her breathing. An hour bundled up playing in the snow and she would begin to cough and wheeze. Twenty minutes at a tree farm in December to get our Christmas tree led to an emergency room visit.

So without warning, without notice or any way to prepare, my life changed completely. Having a medically fragile child is living with the constant fear that today might be the last day God allows you to have them. "Fear is the unwelcome guest that rides on love's new wings," I wrote in a poem when Isaiah was born. But that fear is intensified a thousand times when love's wings are fragile and must be held together with surgical tape and IV tubes.

Looking back, I now cherish those nights I had with Shaylah, holding her and telling her stories to encourage her to breathe the albuterol-laced air from her humming nebulizer. She would panic when she would get short of breath, and her beautiful blue eyes would fill with terror. I would hold her in one arm, hold the nebulizer mask in the other hand, and sing to her above the hum of the motor and the hiss of the medicated mist. Her tiny body would start to relax after a few minutes of the nebulizer, and although the albuterol would make her heart race and agitate her nervous system, the fact that she could breathe would help her to calm down.

I'd sing the same songs I sang to Sonny when we were sitting by a campfire or curled up in a sleeping bag under the stars. I'd make up the same silly "Mike the Mountain Monster" stories that I once shared with her big brother, only instead of a little boy with big brown eyes and soft brown skin being the star of the story, it was a little girl with big blue eyes and soft, soft skin who would go on adventures. When Sonny was small, Mike the Mountain Monster stories would be woven around a mountain hike that led to the lair of a dragon's who was his secret friend. He and I would climb upon Mike's back and soar above the world—oftentimes we would go to California to visit Sonny's dad. Because he missed his father, I would weave stories of trips with his dad to Disneyland, Mike sitting atop Magic Mountain while Sonny and George rode the Disney train around the park. When Isaiah was an adult, a father to his own children, we planned a trip to a Disney park. While planning Isaiah asked how old he was when he went to Disney with his dad. I told him he was about ten months old, the summer my brother disappeared. We took Sonny and his stepsiblings to Disney just weeks before George moved out of our family home. "No," he said. "I was older—I remember riding the train around the park with Dad." As he described his memories with his father, I started to smile and then laugh.

"Do you remember how you got to California to be with your dad?" I asked. He pondered and searched his memory, and when he came up blank, I told him the only trips he made with his dad were to Oregon. The trips to Disney, to Knott's Berry Farm, to the North Pole, and to the mountaintops that he took with his dad were flying on the back of Mike the Mountain Monster.

Shaylah loved the stories as much as her brother did. But hers were told for a different reason. I wove together stories for Sonny to help him feel connected to a father who was too wrapped up in his career and too impaired by his alcoholism to stay connected to his son. For Shaylah, those stories took her out of her bedroom or her hospital bed, away from the humming machines and the IV drips, away from welts and rashes, away from the fear of her throat closing down and out into the world that she was unable to enjoy. I signed her up for swimming lessons as a child, but the chlorine in the pool was too strong and caused her to have an asthma attack. I signed her up for ballet lessons, but the chalk dust in the studio was choking. Hiking, camping, dirt biking were out of the question.

When Shaylah was about four, she started to develop round sores that would not heal on her arms and legs. More trips to the asthma and allergy specialist, more tests, and the doctors decided she was basically allergic to her own body. She would scratch her skin while she was sleeping, and the sores would become infected. Antibiotics and steroids were prescribed to heal the sores, but the antibiotics would make her resistant to medication when she would get pneumonia. Which happened nearly every winter.

Now I realize that my carefree years with Sonny were a gift, and my endless nights holding Shaylah were a gift as well. Had she not prepared me to take care of medically fragile children and to face the reality of the possibility of death, I could not have faced the challenges of most of my adoptive children. Most are medically fragile or have been mentally and physically abused, or all of the above. I certainly could not have adopted kids that I knew were chronically ill, and I never would have fought to bring my son Sammy home.

In 1984, I started a "love songs and requests" show called *Lights Out* from Seattle, Washington. The show was incredibly successful and I enjoyed number-one ratings for a few years before I was fired, again. Seattle was, at the time, the thirteenth-ranked city in America for radio. I dreamed of being like Wolfman Jack or Larry King, syndicated radio personalities broadcasting across the country.

In 1990 my son, Isaiah, and I moved to Boston, ranked number six for radio in the nation. There my special format became simply *The Delilah Show*, where I took phone calls and dedications and spun sappy love songs and shared advice at night. Again we had amazing ratings. I constantly talked to the management about syndicating my show, but their focus was on the Boston market, and they didn't own stations in but two other cities. In 1992 Greater Media, a bigger broadcast company, offered me the opportunity to move to Philadelphia. At the time Philly was the fourth-largest radio market, behind New York, LA, and Dallas. I was eager to continue growing my success, and damn, I loved Philly cheesesteaks!

From 1992 to 1994, the show did well. I got married to my husband Doug, and I bought a small home in a wonderful neighborhood on the Main Line in Radnor Township. Sonny loved it; it came with six other boys his age in the neighborhood and a soccer field at the end of our street. While in my seventh month of pregnancy carrying Shaylah, I flew back to Philly from a visit to Seattle. It was my husband's twenty-sixth birthday, July 11, 1994.

My friend Judy met me at the airport, and after a long, awkward hug that felt like someone had died and a comment about my swollen ankles, Judy schlepped my bags to her car. Judy is Jewish, and very funny. Normally she would be cracking herself up with a dozen one-liners, but on this afternoon she was oddly quiet.

Judy said she had directions to take me to a nice restaurant on the Main Line to have dinner with the management from my station. I argued with her and insisted she take me straight to the station. I had less than an hour to prepare for my show and had lots to catch up on with my producer/roommate, Janey. Again, Judy said she had to take me to the restaurant and again I argued… her face was pale and drawn, and she looked at me and said, "I can't say anything more." I reached up and switched on her radio to my station. As God would have it a sweeper ran, a prerecorded message with zings and swooshes and a booming radio-style voice saying, "The all-new WMGK, all seventies hits, all the time," swish, bam into the Hall and Oates hit "She's Gone." In that instant I knew why Janey hadn't returned my many calls the day before and why Judy avoided eye contact in the terminal.

All seventies, all the time. Overnight they had switched to a disco format and the entire staff was let go.

Judy drove me to the restaurant in silence and said she'd take my bags home. I waddled into the cool air of the well-appointed restaurant, greeted by a lovely, thin girl who looked as though she had never sweated a day in her life, wearing a crisp, straight black dress. My feet were so swollen I was wearing jellies, cheap plastic shoes that stretched. My waterlogged, fleshy feet pushed through the plastic webs, making my enormous feet look like they had been scored with a butter knife. I was wearing a turquoise maternity sundress, shaped like a beach tent you'd sit under at the Jersey Shore. My fingers, too, were swollen beyond recognition, from the pregnancy, the oppressive heat, scraping wallpaper, painting walls, and the altitude of the plane.

I arrived first and took my place at the quiet table in the corner my bosses had reserved. I saw them pull up in separate cars. I quickly hid behind the large menu and acted as if I were unaware of the two suited men standing before me. Julian, surprised that I had seated myself and already started to order, cleared his throat and pulled up a chair. Sitting down, he said, "Delilah, um, what are you doing?"

Without hesitating I said, "I'm looking for the most expensive items on this menu, because I have the feeling this is my last free meal." They laughed, I laughed, and the awkward moment passed. I ordered steak, lobster, and two virgin strawberry daiquiris.

When I got home, I found my producer Janey, heartsick and scared for me. Julian had called her to find out my flight schedule and told her she could not tell me I was being fired. In his haste, he forgot she worked as my producer. After he told her she could not tell me about the format change, she cleared her throat and said, "Excuse me, are you forgetting I work for you, too?"

"Oh yes," he shot back, "we're letting you go, too," and hung up.

When I called Doug to share the bad news, his only comment was, "Thanks for the birthday present."

On September 28, 1994, my girlfriend Brenda, who had lived with me in Boston, and her husband, Billy, stopped in to visit and spend the night with us on their way to see her family in DC. Brenda was a sweet girl, with long, thick hair, a natural beauty that reminded me of the models who sold Dove soap on TV in the seventies. She had sparkly eyes and a broad, open face. She wore little makeup but was radiantly beautiful and had a laugh that was almost musical. When we were roomies, we worked together for a time at the radio station. She was a salesperson and I was on the air. She worked days and I worked nights, so she helped watch Sonny while I did the show. We would get into long philosophical discussions late into the night when I'd get off the air. She had been raised a Christian but insisted any path was a good path to enlightenment. I was a fairly new Christian, had made my commitment to God four years prior, and was on fire to evangelize the world. I may have been a bit heavy-handed back then and probably did more harm than good in my arguments of theology. But for some reason, Brenda listened and let my words challenge her. Later on, she had an experience that touched her on a profound level, and apart from our friendship, she gave her heart to Christ.

So in God's perfect timing, Brenda arrived in Philly on the twenty-eighth of September, planning to leave the next day. We talked late into the night and went to bed. The next morning when I woke up to shower, I found I was lying in a pool of water. My water had broken.

Brenda and Janey excitedly helped me pack, and Doug frantically drove us to the birthing center. I walked around the floor, and we sang praise songs and talked. Janey walked with me, then Brenda, then both girls. Doug took a turn or two, and then the girls took over. From noon till seven or eight we walked and sang and I ate cheese balls. An entire can of cheese balls. My legs were exhausted, my contractions weren't doing much, and I felt like my baby was never going to arrive. I sat down to watch a Disney movie and, finally, the contractions started doing their job.

At 11:47 my baby girl entered the world, fist first! Janey assisted, Brenda sang songs and prayed, a wonderful delivery room nurse named Jane coached, encouraged, and joined us in prayer, and the most beautiful angel I had ever seen became my joy.

Before Brenda left she put me in touch with Ken Spitzer, her former boss at the station we had worked at together. He left a few weeks before I had arrived. Ken was with a new broadcast company, and Brenda shared how badly I wanted to be syndicated.

Over the next few weeks, I nursed my baby and reconciled with my mom, whom I had stopped talking to a few years before, then welcomed her with open arms to my home in Philly. She came for a week and stayed for a month. Mom was a big woman, over six feet tall, and she had a big personality. She had somehow mellowed and whether it was her new granddaughter or something else, she was more sentimental and supportive, less controlling. We had the best time of our lives as mom and daughter. I had been gone from home sixteen years already. I had bought four houses and half a dozen cars, given birth to a son and a daughter, started a street ministry, worked at nine radio stations, and been married three times. But before that visit, Mom always treated me like I was a knucklehead, incapable of paying a bill or driving a car. Or at least that was my perception of how she treated me.

When my mom arrived in Philly, her energy was different. She loved Janey, and she was eager to hear about

Point Hope and the homeless folks we met. She was eager to relax and be spoiled; she let me take her first to DC for a day of sightseeing and then later to New York City. She didn't hijack the trips and insert her own agenda, she didn't snark at me about my weird friends or my bad parenting, she just had fun and laughed with me each night. In DC she laughed when I walked barefoot, nursing my newborn daughter, through the White House and the Capitol building. In New York she laughed at the crazy tour guide Maryanne who slid around the pole on the front of the double-decker tour bus like an aging stripper and greeted us with, "It's *Fri*-dayyy, welcome to Manhattan, the smallest but tallest borough of New York." Her heavy Bronx accent was delightful as she pointed out where Bogie and Bacall had their love nest, and where Frank Sinatra and his Italian friends went for drinks.

She agreed to go with me to the church at Times Square, a very enthusiastic church in a refurbished theater in Times Square. Mom had been adamantly against first my brother Matt's conversion to Christianity, then mine and my younger brother Tim's. I braced myself for her criticism of the evangelical church, but instead she tapped her foot then stood and clapped her hands while recording artist Larnelle Harris led us in worship for nearly an hour. I was shocked, Janey was shocked, Shaylah kept throwing up, and Sonny slept through most of the service.

Mostly Mom adored Shaylah, held her and stared at her for hours, marveling over her dainty hands and her tiny, slim fingers. As a newborn Shay had an air of feminine loveliness about her, the way she held her delicate hands and waved them as if she were a ballet dancer. Sonny adored his baby sister as well and rushed home from school to cuddle and hold her. My heart was full and content during that fall, and driving Mom to the airport as the last brilliant colors of autumn fell in the Philly wind and rain was the hardest thing I had ever done. I sobbed, she bawled, and we clung to each other at the gate. I watched her get on the plane and nearly collapsed with grief. Janey kept saying, "She's coming back, she said she'd be back in the spring," but I had the most ominous premonition, and a haunting, hollow loneliness.

Before Mom left she had heard me talking to Ken Spitzer and believed that maybe I wasn't so crazy for pursuing my radio dreams. Ken had a lot of friends in broadcasting and even more in the financial world, and was fairly certain he could help me get syndicated.

If she were alive today, my mom would probably have a fit at all the kids I've adopted and all the projects I am involved in, but she would fiercely defend me to anyone who tried to stand in my path or stop me. I honestly believe the reason my show went into syndication when it did—five months after her passing—was because she was in heaven nagging God to give me a break. I know the Lord could not resist those green eyes and that broad smile, and I suspect she said something like, "Listen, Lord, Sis has worked hard, and You know she loves what she does. I tried to talk her into getting a real job, but she refused to listen. God, can You just move a few mountains and let this syndication dream come true for her?"

Mom left us in the fall of '95, but before she died she sent a card to my roommate and producer for the past twenty-five years, Janey, and in it she wrote, "I will see you in the spring, when God makes all things new again." In the spring of '96, our show finally went into syndication.

Whatever you are going through today, whatever is happening right now to challenge your well-being and your sanity, you will get past it. You have the strength to endure any challenge you face. If you believe God placed you on this Earth, then you should also believe you have a purpose in this life as you stand here today. You may recognize the saying "If God brought you to it, he'll bring you through it." Believe that.

Some of the hardest, most painful moments in my life have been dealing with the health issues and trauma inflicted on my children. I can't adequately describe how heartbreaking it is to worry in agony over a child. If you're a parent who's been there, you know. But the reality is we all agonize over something at some point in our lives. There will always be trouble in the world, but take heart—Jesus conquered it, and so will you. You have to experience the lows to appreciate the highs. I probably wouldn't appreciate where I am today if I didn't have to work so damn hard and endure so much pain to get here. And I probably wouldn't know half as many things today if I didn't have to learn them the hard way.

When I was battling my daughter's severe health issues, and when I was wayward in my career, it was hard to see past the trouble. When you're enshrouded in stress and uncertainty, there is no joy to be had. But the winter seasons of your life will pass, and God will make all things new again, as my mother, Wilma Dean, professed in her letter to Janey.

Today my daughter is a beautiful woman with a bright future. I see the pain of her own health struggles being redirected into a compassion and nurturing for others. Today I run my own company and my own NGO—no longer can I be fired! And speaking of my mom, I'd like to point out that within the depths of my uncertainty for my future and my family, God brought her back into my life and made that relationship new again. Old wounds were bound as my mom finally believed in me, and I could finally mend her broken heart.

I left home the day I graduated from high school. I didn't ever go back to live at home again, and I never looked back. My little brother would call me at night and beg me to come home; Mom would call me crying and sobbing, telling me how much she missed me. I didn't care. My heart was hardened because of the fights I had with my dad, and I had a chip on my shoulder a mile wide. It wasn't until I had my first child that I realized how I broke her heart by leaving so soon, no transition, no time to adjust to the void in her life. One day I was standing on a wooden stage getting my high school diploma, and the next day I took a suitcase full of clothes and five thousand dollars I had saved and hidden under a loose floorboard in my closet and I left.

When my firstborn son left home, he only moved next door, and still I missed seeing his sleepy face in the morning. Suddenly the weight of how deeply I broke my mom's heart was a reality, and why she had fought to retain her hold on Matt when he and Anne started to get serious. She died long before I fully realized the sacrifices she made to raise me, or how deeply she loved me. Certainly, I didn't realize how I had broken her heart on many occasions by my impetuous or spontaneous decisions, nor did I have time to apologize.

My mom coming back into my life after a new baby, during a rocky relationship and stressful job situation, was the silver lining, a gift. I don't know to whom it meant more, but it is one of the great blessings of my life to this day. It was a rainbow in the midst of the storm. Now when I look back, I realize it was God's way of showing me how He works all things for good, and that it would all eventually be okay.

God will do that, you know. He will deliver the tools or the people to give you strength to press on. That's how much He believes you can survive it, build strength from it, and emerge with a heart to change the world for one person, or many. But change the world, nonetheless.

CHAPTER 13:
A STRENGTHENED HEART

My brother Matt had found his way to a very strong faith before I did. It wasn't a cosmic realization, an awakening, or a spiritual journey he went on to become a Christian. To be honest, it was a tall, blonde girl whose ample assets caught his attention. Anne was cute, with a nose that turned up slightly to give her a somewhat pixie look. They were in a jazz band together at their community college, and when my awkward, gangly, seventeen-year-old brother got up the courage to ask her out, she initially turned him down.

Anne and her family were religious—they were Christians—and though she had a crush on Matt, she wasn't interested in dating a boy who didn't share her faith. I think Matt's conversion had little to do with the scriptures or divine revelation... but convert he did, even as our family smirked and mocked his newfound faith. Especially me.

Matt and Anne dated for a year before he got her the first promise ring and they started to discuss marriage. My parents, especially my mother, were against it. Matt was her firstborn, her baby, and she was not going to give him up easily. Both sets of parents encouraged them to let Matthew finish his education first. Anne waited patiently as he enrolled in Oregon State University through the ROTC program, and she worked at a bank to help support his efforts. A year or so later, he added a small engagement ring to the promise ring, and again my mom had a fit. Finally, after about four years of dating, they announced they would be getting married in the summer of 1981. Again, Mom protested and started to list the reasons they needed to wait.

Anne, usually somewhat of a wallflower, stood up from the kitchen table and said, "Mrs. Luke, I have waited for your son for several years now. I am not going to wait any longer. We are getting married whether you like it or not."

Anne and her mom planned a simple but beautiful wedding. She wore a cotton gown and decorated her church with yellow and white daisies. She married my brother on July 11, 1981. I pinned a boutonniere on my dad before the wedding, and it was the last time I remember touching or hugging him.

When I returned to Seattle after Matt's wedding, I moved in with my new boyfriend George, who was intoxicating, handsome, charming, and brilliant. He was also intoxicated. The first night I met him and pretty much every night after that, he was drunk. But I didn't see a problem with his drinking, as he only became more engaging and affectionate as he drank.

I wasn't used to mean or unruly drunks—I had been raised in a family of people who drank nearly every day, and I loved those people! My folks and all their best friends drank in the evening and usually tied one on every weekend. But these people were funny, loving, larger-than-life folks when they drank. I was never beaten, abused, or left out in the cold when my parents drank. I loved them when they drank even more.

Dad's music was better, and his jokes were funnier; his friends would erupt in volcanic laughter as they sat around the campfire drinking Black Velvet whisky and playing the guitar. Mom's best friend Doris was a gorgeous woman with a long neck and hair that was always teased into a frothy do! She held her cigarette between long thin fingers, her nails were always polished, and she would tip her head back and blow out smoke in a way that made her look sexy as hell. If I ever had a girl crush, it was on Doris!

Being around such funny, engaging adults who drank prepared me to fall in love with a funny, engaging man who drank. Like my dad and his friends, George could operate on all cylinders even after drinking half a bottle of whiskey and a six-pack of beer. In recovery groups the term *functioning alcoholics* is bandied around. But my parents and my first husband weren't just functioning—they were hysterically funny and hardworking. They weren't slackers who hung out in dimly lit bars or slept on park benches, who showed up late to work or couldn't keep a job. I had no issue with the volume of alcohol my beloved consumed when I fell in love with him. Nope, never saw it as a problem in the early days of true love's haze...

If you've watched the Barbra Streisand movie *Funny Girl*, then you saw our story. (Well, except the character played by Barbra Streisand was incredibly funny, talented, and a Broadway star; I was just a girl trying to make it big in radio.) George was so much like Omar Sharif's character in the movie—debonair, suave, and oh so emotionally unavailable.

The hot summer night I met George, a news reporter from another Seattle radio station, I was at a media event for the Seattle Mariners MLB team, and I was seated at a table with a dozen other broadcasters. I saw him standing at the door; my heart jumped out of my chest and into his hands. It was love at first sight. But I may have missed a few road signs that night as we chatted away in the press box while he pounded back half a dozen large plastic cups of beer.

A week before Christmas 1981 and five months after my older brother's wedding, George and I strolled hand in hand in the lightly falling snow and bought a small Christmas tree beneath the buzzing streetlights on Harbor Avenue and carried it to our apartment that smelled of barbecue and weed. After we decorated the four-foot-high Douglas fir with ornaments, George got down on one knee, put a minuscule diamond ring on my left hand, and asked me to marry him. He neglected to mention he was still very married to another woman, six years behind in child support payments, and hadn't filed taxes for at least five years. He also collected women's phone numbers like I collected Journey albums, and he loved to party and get high with his friends. I missed these signs and many more, but I loved him something awful, and there was no snapping me out of it.

We were married on a Saturday in September 1982 in a park overlooking Seattle. Only sixteen people were at our wedding. My father had forbidden anyone in my family to attend, so he and my mother, sister, and little brother were absent. Only Matt and Anne, who had an independent life in California, were there to represent my family. My two best girlfriends from childhood, Natasha and Dee Dee, were there, along with a few work friends and some folks I had met in Seattle. I made my satin wedding dress from a McCall's pattern; it had spaghetti straps with a little jacket to match. I made dresses for Tash and Dee and for my stepdaughter, Camille. I even sewed a vest for my stepson, Adrian, to wear. I made the bouquets for me and the girls to carry, plus half a dozen corsages, boutonnieres, and the flowers that were tied to the cake knife.

George's insanely funny younger brother, Mike, was in charge of the music for the ceremony. Holding on to my brother Matt's arm, I walked beneath climbing roses and entered the little gathering at the park. The music recorded on a cassette tape was supposed to be our song, "Always and Forever" by Heatwave. Instead, Mike forgot to take his personal tape out of the boom box, so I walked down the grassy aisle on my brother's arm to Kool and the Gang's "Get Down on It"! Everyone laughed at the irony as we tied the knot with the city spread out like a magic carpet below us.

The sun danced off the inky-blue waters of Puget Sound, birds flew overhead, George's two beautiful children held my hand, and my heart nearly exploded with joy. It truly was the happiest day of my life, and I knew he would love and adore only me now that we were married. He promised to do so in the tender vows he wrote and spoke to me in his deep tenor voice. He promised to love, honor, and cherish only me... "And when the dark dog of despair comes howling at our door, as it will in life at times, I will protect you from all harm and hold you until the morning light."

A year later we went on a delayed honeymoon to Mexico. After a very large margarita, I told George I wanted a baby and if he didn't want another child, he would have to do something to prevent it. I flicked my wrist as I threw my birth control pills in the garbage can of the Siesta Royale. Within a few weeks, I was pregnant. But instead of being as elated as I was, George was frustrated and upset. I had no clue when I called him at work to tell him the good news that Rose, the woman who answered the phone in their newsroom, was in fact sleeping with him.

He came home and gently tried to tell me I needed to abort the baby; he confessed that he was not a good father to the two children he had, that he neglected his responsibilities to them and he felt bad for that. I couldn't believe what he was saying. I knew he would be a great daddy, that we loved each other so much he would change, that he would stop going out after work and drinking every night, stop heading to the clubs on weekends with the boys. I knew the two other wives he had wed before me had simply not understood him nor loved him as much as I did.

When he realized I wasn't going to change my mind, he actually changed his—his mood became acceptance, followed by happiness, even animation in the following months about our unborn baby. I was so happy, so intoxicated on love and joy knowing there was a little "us" growing inside me, I convinced myself our fights and problems were a thing of the past and we would have the most adorable, loving family in the history of families.

I had purchased a modest house—they call them war boxes in West Seattle, little shacks that were built during World War II for all the civilians who worked at the shipyards and Boeing field. I planted flowers and trees in our front yard, dug up the sod and put a garden in the backyard. I put a white picket fence around the whole lovely lot. I sewed curtains for the baby's room, the living room, the bedrooms. I worked at a radio station part-time and a video production company during the week, working four months straight without a single day off. Working, digging, planting, painting, sewing, and rubbing my growing belly, I was so stinking happy my face hurt from smiling.

Our amazing son was born at 3:22 on a warm September afternoon. I had to beg George to turn off the TV—the Seattle Seahawks were set to play the New England Patriots, and he was well into his second six-pack of Henry's Private Reserve when my contractions became unbearable. It wasn't until I stood in front of our fourteen-inch TV and screamed at him that it wasn't false labor, as the fluid ran down my swollen legs, that he abandoned the game and drove me to the birthing center in Redmond, half an hour away.

When I got to the hospital, they said the baby was in distress and his heart rate was slowing down, so they prepped me and did an emergency C-section within a few minutes of our arrival. So much for my birthing plan. I had envisioned listening to deep-breathing exercises, relaxing to James Taylor, lighting aromatic candles, and having an underwater delivery in the birthing center's new soaking tub. Instead they rushed me in, gave me an epidural, cut me open, and then placed my beautiful baby boy in my arms. Isaiah entered the world at almost nine pounds, and the world as I had known it came to an immediate end. My life was divided into before and after Isaiah was born. My son's birth was the earth-shattering event that changed everything. Rearranged my psyche and put me in touch with the infinite.

I honestly had no clue how much my mom loved me until Isaiah was born, no clue the level of love I was capable of experiencing, sharing, or giving until he came into my life. And it was by holding him, nursing him, and caring for him that I began to comprehend what my brother had tried to share with me the last time we talked—that there is a heaven, a purpose, a plan, and a God that is real.

$$\sim$$

Many years ago, a pastor named Mike McCorkle shared a few simple thoughts with me and the rest of our tiny congregation; he said he believed when he arrives in heaven, God will ask him two questions. The first will be, "What did you do with Me—did you get to know Me?" God will want to know if you had a relationship with Him. The second will be, "What did you do with every person I placed in your path?"

I don't know if that will happen or not. I haven't a clue if God will ask me those two questions, or if something entirely different will transpire when my heart stops beating and my life ebbs away. But what if Pastor Mike was right? What if God wasn't kidding about the "Judge ye not" thing and wants me to love others instead of judge them? What if he is serious about that "Do unto others as you would have done unto you" part? What if every single person in my life, from my hardheaded, stubborn father to my tenderhearted firstborn son, every person I served a sandwich to on the street or every person whose call I took on the air, was placed in my life by God and I was supposed to impact their life for good? What if God means it when He tells us to love the unlovely? What if life is more than random coincidences and chance meetings? What if He actually orchestrates the people we encounter? What if there is a grand plan to things and He is putting people in my path to connect with, appreciate, and even love? What if?

These thoughts could not leave my mind. I was in my twenties and searching for answers, having lost my brother Matt and his wife, Anne, in a tragic plane crash.

After graduating from college with a civil engineering degree, Matt attended Officer Candidate School and graduated with the rank of second lieutenant in the US Air Force. He was stationed at Vandenberg AFB near Lompoc, California, and assigned the exciting task of re-engineering the base sewer and drainage system. Anne, his wife of nearly four years, worked at a local bank, and there was a lot of talk about them becoming parents.

Once comfortably installed on base, Matt set out to realize his lifelong dream of becoming a pilot. Flight had been his passion for as long as anyone could remember; he had spent countless hours as a youth and teen building and flying model aircraft, and he wanted to be a military pilot. Unfortunately, his six-foot-five-inch height had prevented this, but he now had the time and the means to pursue a private pilot's license, and he did. Anne attended ground school so she could be his handy copilot on the many airborne adventures they dreamed of taking.

They set off from Vandenberg on their first flight together the Wednesday before Memorial Day weekend in 1985, en route to North Bend, Oregon, to visit both sets of parents. From there they were to fly to Seattle to meet their new nephew and godson, Isaiah, now eight months. Bad weather met them, and they landed in Redding and camped in a tent under the plane on the tarmac that night. The next morning, Thursday, they were cleared for takeoff, but the rain and fog pursued them. Matt was not yet instrument rated, so he tried to get below the cloud cover and follow the Umpqua River west toward the coast. He had contact with the small airport tower in Roseburg, Oregon, before heading west, and that was the last anyone heard his voice. They vanished into the clouds. Gone. Ground and air search teams found no trace. On the second day of the search, a Civil Air Patrol plane crashed, killing all three volunteers on board. Our family was shattered.

It was Matt's accident and the horrific pain that tore my heart out each day thereafter that led me on my spiritual journey. It was his passing that ultimately led me to

West Seattle Free Methodist Church, and then to my faith in the Lord.

Listening to this particular two-part sermon on God's will, I went through a frustrating time. I tried to convince myself that Pastor Mike was mistaken. That there was no cosmic plan or design to the people I encountered each day. It was unthinkable that each person was placed in my path on purpose; even more impossible to grasp was this notion that I was to respond to them with real love. I'm a very friendly person, and I've always been affectionate and demonstrative—*to the people I like.* It was the notion that I was to love those I didn't like that I couldn't stop thinking about.

Did God really want me to love my ex-husband, who had walked out of our lives as blithely as he had walked in? Did God really want me to love those who were just unlikable? The annoying kid who raised his hand in an obnoxious way, waving it around, hoping the teacher would call on him? "Shut up, Terry," my internal voice would say each time he awkwardly thrust his fleshy hand upward, and mentally I would slap it down. He annoyed me; I have no clue why, but he did. So do a lot of people. Maybe you have people who annoy you, disappoint you, dislike you—neighbors who constantly fight and whose dog barks all night, people who pretend to care but stab you in the back the first chance they get. Ex-lovers who talk about you in disparaging ways, ex-friends who broke up with you and didn't offer an explanation.

People who listen to my show or meet me at an appearance, who write to me on social media or to the radio stations, think I'm always nice, always patient, always soft-spoken. I'm not. At all. I have a hard time forgiving people who have hurt me or wronged me, a hard time putting up with people who are ignorant or foolish. Who demand they be listened to and respected, but do not extend that courtesy to anyone who disagrees with them. I get annoyed and mentally slap their hand or the back of their head.

But what if Pastor Mike was right? How do you love someone you hate? Someone who has harmed you to the core of your being? Someone who is just not likable?

Well, to begin with, I had to learn what God means when He says to love our enemies. To forgive those who persecute us. It is impossible to love someone who has wounded you until you can forgive them. And it is impossible to forgive someone who has wronged you until you understand the nature of forgiveness in God's eyes.

First, you must get honest and define why someone is your enemy. And that means getting real about what happened. The saying "We are only as sick as our secrets" comes into play once again. Find someone safe, a pastor or a counselor or a best friend, and share the secrets. If you can't speak them to anyone, write it down. Write what happened to you, and as you write, more will come to you. Do *not* write it down to hurt someone else, or to wound the person who wounded you. Write it down to get it out of your head. If you don't get it out of your head, you will eventually go out of your head.

As you write your story, own it, and eventually share it, the pain loses its power over you. You can stop being the victim and become the victorious. Through sharing, you will find others who have similar experiences, and together you can strengthen one another and learn to walk in the light instead of hiding in darkened shadows. I have heard that most addictions and many mental illnesses have their root in these hidden secrets from our past. That our addictive behaviors are often self-medicating to try to escape the pain of secrets we feel are too dark to share.

Once the pain has lost its power over you, then you take the next step—to forgive the person or institution that wronged you. How? It's simple, but not easy. Forgiveness does not mean you deny the abuse or the injustice, and it does not mean you accept the abuse or the injustice as acceptable behavior. To forgive doesn't mean you accept some of what happened or compare your story to someone else's story. A lot of people I know, when they begin the healing journey, they compare or contrast their experience to others' and say, "Well, I guess my pain wasn't so bad. You had it a lot worse." You will always meet people who had it worse, and people who suffered much less than you did; it doesn't matter. Your pain is your pain, your story is your story. Own it but don't make excuses for the person who wronged you, and don't convince yourself what you experienced was in any way acceptable or okay.

When it comes to the actual act of forgiveness, what has worked for me is to envision a big basket full of pain, anger, and wounds in my arms. In my mind's eye, I place this basket full of pain labeled "uncollected debts" into God's lap. And any time I start to feel that rage rising up inside, I mentally and prayerfully place it back into God's hands.

When I first started doing this exercise, I would envision God pummeling those who had wronged me. I fantasized about God's wrath being poured out like hot oil upon their heads. But as time passes and I see these same people suffering, I start to feel compassion, even sorrow, for them. The anger that once weighed me down turns to prayers that God will lift them up and heal them. That is how God works to redeem our pain and suffering into a miraculous shift of strength and compassion.

Now that your arms have been emptied of the uncollected debts, anger, and pain, you are ready to use them for a greater purpose. You've made room to fill those arms with people who come into your life. Now that you have poured the bitterness out of your soul upon the ground of God's mercy, you are ready to be filled with the purpose you were designed for.

And you will indeed be on your way to answering those two questions Pastor Mike has set before us: What did you do with God, and what did you do with the people He placed in your life? The answer may simply be that you used one to love the other.

$$\sim$$

This book is my story. Just a handful of stories, actually. There are plenty more where these came from. But I handpicked a few that illustrate a bit of my journey to now, how I got where I am, who influenced me (whether for bad or good, but always for growth), and how my faith in God was made stronger through it all. When I look back, I can see the divine knitting together of these moments in my life, people in my life, lessons in my life. And if you listen to me on air, hearing a bit of wisdom come from my lips, well, now you know where it comes from. It comes from living, it comes from loving and learning; it comes from failing and falling, and it often has come from picking myself up off the ground.

I've lost a great deal in my life. I've lost the lives of people I cherished, and I've lost the lives of people with whom I didn't get to bind old wounds. I've lost husbands, I've lost friends, I've lost wayward children. I've lost job after job after job. I've seen addiction destroy lives, rip families apart. I've seen children die of hunger. I've seen people die from painful, horrible diseases in third-world countries. I've seen children torn from abusive family situations and put into other abusive homes. I've been witness to some pretty harsh things in life. It's enough to question how a God of the universe can exist. With all this trouble in the world, what's the point?

I want you to know this: the God of the universe is why you are here on this earth at this moment. The things of this world may pass away, but He is forever. Your loved ones may pass away like mine have, but they pass right back into the arms of their Creator, and only we are left to grieve. Those beautiful African children I cry for and pray over, when they die in my arms, I know their perfect souls go on to dance in heaven.

There may not be a win to counter every loss or hardship we experience in life, but there is always a comeback. Don't count your losses in life—count your comebacks. There is a verse in the Bible that says, "The Lord himself goes before you and will be with you." By this alone, you can take comfort in knowing your path has already been paved and your comebacks have already been designed. We were not created for failure... let that sink into your heart for a minute. Every life, short as it may be, has a purpose on this planet. And every person you encounter on this planet probably has a purpose in your life.

As long as you're living and breathing, let's amend Pastor Mike's second question to ask, "What can you do with the people God has placed in your life going forward?" You can't change the past, but you can take hold of your future. You can love people, you can forgive them— we've gone over that. Have you also considered that God places people in your life to do something for you? Perhaps to love you, to teach you something... perhaps to grow your patience. Not everyone we meet is meant to be someone we adore, let's get real. Perhaps some people are meant to help us learn a lesson, albeit a painful one. I learned several hard lessons from my marriage to my ex-husband George, but I also got the gift of my amazing firstborn son, and a seed of faith in the divine planted in my heart on the day of his birth. Beauty for ashes.

CONCLUSION

A lot has changed since I was that little girl who begged my mom to sew a coat for Kathy at the bus stop, since I was that fourth-grade girl who wanted to help orphans in Vietnam. My world has gotten a lot bigger since then. I've made a lot of foolish choices, and I've been the victim of other people's foolish choices, too. But in reality, those choices all led me down a path of understanding the human frailties that God puts in front of me each day. It's allowed me to find the good in people, even when they've done bad things. It's allowed me to be a sounding board for people in all different walks of life. I've come to accept who I am, what I've done; I've owned my mistakes and know for a fact I'll have to own more mistakes yet to be made.

I have been in radio making connections with people for the better part of my life. I've shared bits and pieces of my story on air, and much more off the air. But the blessing for me has been hearing the stories from people who call in. I hear their hearts, and it changes mine. I've been fortunate enough to let some of their words sink in and shift my perspective. It's been a healing therapy for me to listen to stories and reciprocate by sharing my own experiences. Unfortunately, most of these extended caller conversations happen later on and never get broadcast.

My point is these circular conversations and stories are healthy; the connections that are made, even during a brief call with a stranger, in my case, can be life-changing. Have you ever had an aha moment when someone says something so simple but so profound? It's kind of like that. You only get those moments when you share your story with someone who can share back.

This life is hard. There is a lot going on in the world today that makes it even harder. And I believe that's why now, more than ever, we need to be sounding boards for each other. Maybe that looks like joining or organizing a parents' group, a support group, a church group, a book club, a walking club, a volunteer organization... Maybe that looks like inviting a friend who may be down and out for coffee and a vent session. My heart is for making connections with people, because as you've read in my stories, you never know how far one of those connections might take you.

It's all planned, my friends. Your stories, your comebacks, and your connections with people. What it comes down to now is simply opening your heart to all of the possibilities God has in store for you. I believe in you. I believe I would like to give you a great big hug and say, "You *got* this." I believe your journey, your stories, your battle scars, and your enduring love are uniquely appointed to help change this world for good, one heart at a time. *It starts with yours...*

ACKNOWLEDGMENTS

I'd like to express my gratitude to the many people who saw me through this book, to all those who provided support, talked things over, read, wrote, offered comments, allowed me to use their stories, and assisted in the editing, proofreading, and design.

My sister, friend, and digital content director, DeAnna Luke, for her insights, memories, and creative input. Her sleuthing skills and passion for the historical truth of our family tree and her sense of humor are always spot-on. Although we have the same DNA, our experiences and relationships within our family were and are vastly different. I know that it was challenging for her to read many of these stories, as she is fiercely protective of not only the family tree, but the nuts that have fallen from it!

Melissa Cudworth and Francine LaSala for their valuable input, and for reading, rereading, probing, and asking good questions, helping me to dig deeper and share more from the heart. Melissa, especially, for her superior organizational skills, which helped to turn my many stories into something that resembles a book!

Kraig Kitchin for being consistent, diligent, and kind when he harps at me to get stories and chapters completed, even if the project was two years over the original deadline!

My thanks to RosettaBooks CEO Arthur Klebanoff, for his tremendous support, as well as Editorial Director Roger Cooper, whose creative spirit greeted me and showed me how welcome authors are at RosettaBooks. As well, my thanks to Hannah Bennett, associate publisher, who shepherded this book through many iterations, and to Chuck Lisberger for introducing me to so many nice people at RosettaBooks.

The people of Africa, my village in Ghana, where I really learned what matters in life, and what is just stuff. My thanks to the Point Hope, Ghana, team; Adam, Tutu, Ida, and all others who have accepted this *obruni* as part of their tribe. To Executive Director Jan Haynes and all Point Hope volunteers for your selfless giving, inexhaustible energies, and lending your voices to the voiceless.

My village here in America, the people who work with me, live with me, care for my kids and my animals, and eat at my table. Kimmy, Joni, Wendi, Dee Dee, Ryan, AlHassan, Joy, Chip, Tim, and dozens of others who bring me such laughter and joy.

To my children, bio, adopted, step, foster, grand, and all who have found their way to my life and stayed for weeks or months… the ones who have grown and are now sharing their own stories and memories with their children, and the ones who are still in the mama bear's den, finding their strengths, talents, and voices. And especially my son Sammy, who now soars and flies with the angels.

Paul, my wonderful husband, who is happy to stand in the shadow and watch me soar, who has glued back all the broken pieces from my past failed marriages and allowed me to be who I am without trying to change, control or diminish my passions.

To God. My Savior, my redeemer, my everything. For Your unfailing love and Your mercies, which are new every morning!

ABOUT THE AUTHOR

Delilah is one of America's most popular radio personalities, and the most listened-to woman on the radio in America. Her self-titled radio program boasts an estimated nine million listeners nationwide. She has been inducted into the National Radio Hall of Fame and the NAB Broadcasting Hall of Fame. Her show's success earned her a National Association of Broadcasters Marconi Award in 2016 as Network/Syndication Personality of the Year, and a GRACIE Award in 2012. Delilah is also the founder of Point Hope, an NGO that champions forgotten children, particularly those in the Ghanaian community

Delilah

Buduburam, as well as those in the American foster care system. The mother of thirteen children, ten of them adopted, Delilah splits her time between her nighttime radio program, trips to Ghana, her fifty-five-acre working farm, and her large family. She is the author of three previous books: *Love Someone Today*, *Love Matters*, and *Arms Full of Love*.